BUENOS AIRES

TRAVEL GUIDE (Full-Color) 2024-2025:

Navigating the Heart of Argentina: A Complete Guide Exploring its Iconic Attractions, Hidden Gems, Maps, Neighborhoods, and Lesser-Known Sides of This Vibrant City.

BY

Lucia E. Garcia

CONTENT

MAP OF BUENOS AIRES

Chapter 1: Introduction to Buenos Aires

Why Visit Buenos Aires in 2024-2025?

Buenos Aires is a city where the energy is palpable and the culture is rich, making it one of South America's must-visit destinations. In 2024-2025, Buenos Aires offers an exciting blend of old-world charm, modern innovation, and cultural vibrancy, making it a perfect time to explore this cosmopolitan city. Here are some compelling reasons to visit during these years:

- **Cultural Festivals and Events**: Buenos Aires is renowned for its cultural events, and 2024-2025 will see a variety of world-class festivals, including the **Buenos Aires International Tango Festival**, the **Buenos Aires International Book Fair**, and the **Carnaval Porteño**. These events offer visitors a deep dive into the city's passion for music, dance, and literature.
- **Tango Renaissance**: As the birthplace of tango, Buenos Aires is continually revitalizing this iconic dance and music style. The city's milongas (tango dance halls) and performances are going through a renaissance, featuring both traditional and modern interpretations that showcase the timeless allure of tango.
- **Renovated Attractions and New Developments**: Several historic landmarks and neighborhoods are undergoing renovations, making them more accessible and appealing to tourists. In addition, new attractions, including contemporary art galleries, boutique hotels, and gourmet dining experiences, are popping up throughout the city.

- **Affordable Travel Destination**: Due to favorable exchange rates, Buenos Aires remains an affordable destination for travelers from many countries. Visitors can experience high-quality dining, entertainment, and accommodations at a fraction of the cost compared to other major cities around the world.
- **A City of Contrasts**: Buenos Aires offers a unique blend of **European elegance** and **Latin American spirit**. Its architecture features French-inspired facades, while its streets are filled with the rhythms of cumbia, rock, and tango. The city's neighborhoods—each with its own character—provide endless exploration opportunities, from the **colorful streets of La Boca** to the upscale boutiques of **Recoleta** and the bohemian charm of **San Telmo**.

A Brief History of Buenos Aires

Buenos Aires has a fascinating history that spans over five centuries, shaping its cultural and social landscape into what it is today. Here's a look at some key moments:

- **Founding and Early History (1536 - 1810)**: Buenos Aires was first founded in **1536** by Spanish explorer **Pedro de Mendoza**, but the original settlement was short-lived due to conflict with local Indigenous peoples. It was refounded in **1580** by **Juan de Garay** and grew as a modest port town. During the colonial period, it became a key trading hub, especially for cattle products like leather and salted meat, despite Spain's restrictive trade policies.
- **Revolution and Independence (1810 - 1880)**: The **May Revolution of 1810** marked the beginning of the struggle for independence from Spain. Buenos Aires played a central role in the **Argentine War of Independence**, which culminated in 1816. In the subsequent decades, political power struggles between the city's elites and rural factions shaped Argentina's development. The late 19th century brought a wave of European immigrants, significantly influencing the city's culture, architecture, and demographics.
- **Economic Boom and European Influence (1880 - 1930)**: Buenos Aires saw tremendous growth during the late 19th and early 20th centuries, fueled by Argentina's agricultural exports. The city's architecture mirrored the **Belle Époque** style of Paris, with grand boulevards and stately mansions. This era left a lasting impact on Buenos Aires' cultural scene, leading to the establishment of iconic venues like the **Teatro Colón**, one of the world's premier opera houses.
- **Political Turmoil and Cultural Transformation (1930 - 1980)**: The 20th century was marked by political instability, economic fluctuations, and social change. The rise of **Juan Domingo Perón** and **Eva Perón** in the 1940s brought significant political shifts, with policies focused on social welfare. The **1950s to the 1980s** were characterized

by military coups, economic challenges, and cultural transformations, with tango evolving from its origins to a symbol of national identity.

- **Modern Era and Revival (1980s - Present)**: Since the return to democracy in **1983**, Buenos Aires has embraced modernization while preserving its cultural heritage. The city's neighborhoods have experienced revitalization, and contemporary cultural movements have flourished. Today, Buenos Aires is a dynamic metropolis where the past and present converge, making it a culturally rich destination with a compelling history.

Buenos Aires Today: Culture, Politics, and Economy

Buenos Aires is a vibrant city with a unique blend of cultural influences, an evolving political landscape, and a dynamic economy. Understanding these aspects is crucial for grasping the essence of the city in 2024-2025.

- **Culture**: As the cultural heart of Argentina, Buenos Aires is a city that lives and breathes art, music, and dance. The city is famous for its **tango heritage**, but its cultural offerings go far beyond, including **theater, literature, visual arts**, and **culinary experiences**. The city's **street art** scene is one of the most prominent in Latin America, reflecting social and political commentary. Buenos Aires is also known for its lively nightlife, where bars, cafes, and nightclubs stay open until the early hours of the morning.
- **Politics**: Buenos Aires, as Argentina's capital, plays a central role in the country's political scene. The city's politics reflect broader national issues, including debates over economic policies, social programs, and governance. In recent years, political discussions have focused on **economic stability, inflation**, and the **preservation of cultural heritage**. The 2024-2025 period may see new political developments as Argentina continues to navigate these challenges.
- **Economy**: The economy of Buenos Aires is diverse, with significant contributions from sectors like **tourism, finance, retail, and technology**. The city's tourism industry is a major economic driver, supported by its rich cultural heritage and numerous attractions. **Agricultural exports** remain vital to the economy, while the **tech startup scene** has been expanding rapidly in recent years. Although Argentina faces economic challenges, such as inflation, Buenos Aires continues to attract international businesses and travelers alike.

How to Use This Guide

This guide is designed to help you make the most of your visit to Buenos Aires in 2024-2025, offering a comprehensive look at everything the city has to offer. Here's how to navigate the guide effectively:

- **Planning Your Trip**: Start with practical information in Chapter 2, covering essential travel tips, entry requirements, currency information, and helpful advice for first-time visitors.
- **Exploring Neighborhoods**: Chapters 5 and 6 dive into the city's neighborhoods and top attractions, providing insights into what makes each area unique. Use these sections to plan your daily itineraries.
- **Cultural Experiences**: Chapter 7 is dedicated to cultural activities, including tango, food, and local traditions. Whether you're looking to attend a tango show or sample traditional Argentine dishes, this chapter will guide you to the best experiences.
- **Dining, Shopping, and Nightlife**: If you're a foodie, shopaholic, or nightlife enthusiast, Chapters 8, 9, and 10 are essential reading. Find the best restaurants, local markets, and entertainment venues to enjoy the city's vibrant atmosphere.
- **Day Trips and Excursions**: Chapter 11 provides information on nearby destinations that can be visited on day trips, such as **Tigre Delta** or **Colonia del Sacramento** in Uruguay. These options are perfect for extending your Buenos Aires experience.
- **Practical Tips and Resources**: For safety advice, transportation details, and other practical matters, refer to Chapter 15. It's packed with useful tips to help you navigate the city comfortably.
- **Interactive Content and Resources**: Use the recommended apps and online resources mentioned throughout the guide to enhance your experience and make travel easier.

With this guide, you'll be well-prepared to experience Buenos Aires to the fullest, whether you're interested in history, culture, food, or just wandering the streets and taking in the sights. Each chapter has been curated to ensure you enjoy a well-rounded and memorable trip to one of Latin America's most captivating cities.

Chapter 2: Planning Your Trip

Planning a trip to Buenos Aires helps you make the most of your visit. Knowing the best time to go, visa rules, currency tips, safety advice, and a bit of the local language will make your trip smoother and more enjoyable. This chapter covers all the basics you need to get ready for your visit.

Best Times to Visit Buenos Aires

Buenos Aires is a great place to visit any time of the year, but the best time depends on what you want to do and what kind of weather you prefer.

- **Spring (September to November)**: Spring is one of the nicest times to visit because the weather is mild (15°C to 25°C / 59°F to 77°F). The parks are full of blooming flowers, especially the purple jacaranda trees, making it perfect for outdoor activities and festivals.
    - **What's Special**: Beautiful parks, fun outdoor events.
    - **Things to Do**: Attend the Buenos Aires International Jazz Festival and see the blooming jacaranda trees.
- **Summer (December to February)**: Summer can get hot and humid, with temperatures reaching 30°C to 35°C (86°F to 95°F). January is quieter since many locals leave for vacation, but it's a lively time for nightlife with lots of outdoor bars and activities.
    - **What's Special**: Busy nightlife, New Year celebrations.
    - **Things to Do**: Watch tango performances outside, visit rooftop bars, and go on beach trips.
- **Autumn (March to May)**: This is another great time to visit because the weather is cooler (13°C to 24°C / 55°F to 75°F) and there are fewer crowds. It's perfect for sightseeing and exploring.
    - **What's Special**: Cooler temperatures, fewer tourists.
    - **Things to Do**: Visit the Buenos Aires International Book Fair and explore museums.
- **Winter (June to August)**: Winter is mild, with temperatures from 8°C to 15°C (46°F to 59°F). It's a good time for indoor activities like museums, theaters, and tango shows.
    - **What's Special**: Cozy cafes, indoor cultural events.
    - **Things to Do**: See a show at Teatro Colón and explore indoor markets.

Visa Requirements and Entry Information

Before traveling to Buenos Aires, check if you need a visa. Here's what you should know:

- **Visa-Free Countries**: Travelers from countries like the **U.S.**, **Canada**, **Australia**, **European Union**, and most South American nations don't need a visa for short visits (usually up to 90 days). Just make sure your passport is valid for at least six months beyond your stay.
- **Visa Required Countries**: Some travelers will need a visa. It's best to contact the nearest Argentine embassy to find out. If you need a visa, you'll usually need a valid passport, a visa application, and proof that you can pay for your stay.
- **Proof of Onward Travel**: You may be asked to show a return ticket or a ticket to another destination when entering Argentina, so keep this information handy.
- **Extending Your Stay**: If you want to stay longer than 90 days, you can apply for an extension at the **Dirección Nacional de Migraciones** office in Buenos Aires.
- **Traveling with Kids**: If traveling with children under 18, you may need extra paperwork, like permission from both parents if the child is traveling alone or with just one parent.

For the latest visa details, visit the official **Argentine Immigration website**: https://www.migraciones.gov.ar.

Currency, Money Exchange, and Tipping Etiquette

The currency in Buenos Aires is the **Argentine peso (ARS)**. Here's what you need to know about managing money and tipping:

- **Currency and Exchange Rates**: The peso's value can change a lot, so check the rate before your trip. You might find better exchange rates on the unofficial market, called the "blue dollar." However, it's safer and legal to use official exchange places like banks or licensed exchange offices, known as "**casas de cambio**."
  - **Airport Exchange and ATMs**: You can change money at **Ezeiza International Airport**, but rates might not be as good. ATMs are common, but they might have withdrawal limits and fees.
  - **Credit and Debit Cards**: While cards are accepted in many places, smaller stores, markets, and some restaurants may prefer cash. Carry some pesos just in case.
- **Tipping Guidelines**:
  - **Restaurants**: Leave about **10%** of the bill as a tip.
  - **Taxis**: It's not expected, but rounding up the fare is appreciated.

- **Hotel Staff**: Tip **50-100 ARS** for porters and **100-200 ARS** for housekeeping per day.
- **Tour Guides**: Tip about **10% to 20%** if the service was good.

Health and Safety Tips for Travelers

Buenos Aires is generally safe, but here are some tips to keep in mind:

- **Health Tips**:
  - **Vaccinations**: No special shots are needed, but it's a good idea to have your routine vaccines (like **measles, tetanus**) up to date. If you plan to visit areas near Brazil, consider getting the **yellow fever vaccine**.
  - **Drinking Water**: Tap water is safe, but some people prefer bottled water.
  - **Pharmacies and Medical Care**: Pharmacies are everywhere, and some stay open late. Buenos Aires has good medical facilities, and many doctors speak English. Make sure you have travel insurance that covers emergencies.
- **Safety Tips**:
  - **Watch Out for Pickpockets**: This can happen in crowded areas, like public transportation or tourist spots. Keep your belongings secure and avoid flashing expensive items.
  - **Common Scams**: Be cautious of strangers who spill something on you and then offer to help clean it off, as they might be trying to steal from you. Politely say no to unexpected help.
  - **Safe and Unsafe Areas**: During the day, most neighborhoods are safe, but at night, be cautious in **La Boca** and parts of **Constitución**. Stick to well-lit, busy streets after dark.
  - **Emergency Numbers**: Call **911** for the police or **107** for medical emergencies.

Language Basics: Essential Spanish Phrases

While many people in Buenos Aires speak English, especially in tourist spots, knowing some basic Spanish will help you enjoy your trip more. Here are some helpful phrases:

- **Common Greetings**:
  - **Hello / Goodbye**: Hola / Adiós
  - **Good morning / Good afternoon / Good evening**: Buenos días / Buenas tardes / Buenas noches
  - **Please / Thank you / You're welcome**: Por favor / Gracias / De nada
  - **Excuse me (to get attention) / I'm sorry**: Disculpe / Lo siento
- **Asking for Directions**:

- **Where is…?**: ¿Dónde está…?
- **How do I get to…?**: ¿Cómo llego a…?
- **Is it near / far?**: ¿Está cerca / lejos?
- **At a Restaurant**:
    - **Can I have the menu, please?**: ¿Me trae el menú, por favor?
    - **I would like…**: Me gustaría…
    - **The bill, please**: La cuenta, por favor
    - **Is there a vegetarian option?**: ¿Hay una opción vegetariana?
- **Shopping**:
    - **How much does this cost?**: ¿Cuánto cuesta esto?
    - **Can you give me a discount?**: ¿Me puede hacer un descuento?
- **Emergency Phrases**:
    - **I need help**: Necesito ayuda
    - **Call the police / doctor**: Llame a la policía / Llame al doctor
    - **I am lost**: Estoy perdido/a

Knowing a few phrases and using a language app like **Duolingo** or **Google Translate** can help you get around and make a good impression with locals.

Chapter 3: Getting to Buenos Aires

Buenos Aires is one of South America's most iconic cities, renowned for its culture, history, and vibrant street life. As Argentina's capital, the city is a central transportation hub, making it accessible from various international and domestic locations. In this chapter, we'll explore the major airports serving the city, airlines and flight routes, practical tips for arrivals, and alternative transportation options such as ferries and buses from neighboring countries.

Major International and Domestic Airports

Buenos Aires is served by two main airports: **Ministro Pistarini International Airport (Ezeiza)** and **Aeroparque Jorge Newbery**, each catering to different types of flights and travelers.

1. **Ministro Pistarini International Airport (Ezeiza)**
   - **Location**: Located about 22 kilometers (14 miles) southwest of downtown Buenos Aires, in the suburb of Ezeiza.
   - **Airport Code**: EZE
   - **Overview**: The primary international gateway to Argentina, Ezeiza handles most long-haul international flights. It has three terminals (A, B, and C) connected by walkways, offering various amenities, duty-free shops, restaurants, and lounges.
   - **Facilities**:
     - **Duty-Free Shopping**: Available in Terminal A, offering a range of luxury goods, cosmetics, and Argentine products like wines and chocolates.
     - **Wi-Fi**: Free internet access throughout the airport.
     - **Currency Exchange**: Several currency exchange services are available, though rates may be more favorable in the city.
     - **Lounges**: VIP lounges such as the **Aeropuertos VIP Club** and **American Express Lounge**.
   - **Website**: Ezeiza Airport
2. **Aeroparque Jorge Newbery (AEP)**
   - **Location**: Situated approximately 2 kilometers (1.2 miles) from the city center, along the Rio de la Plata waterfront.
   - **Airport Code**: AEP
   - **Overview**: This airport primarily serves domestic flights within Argentina and some regional international flights to neighboring countries like Uruguay,

Brazil, and Chile. Its proximity to downtown Buenos Aires makes it a convenient option for travelers connecting within the country.

- ○ **Facilities**:
  - ■ **Restaurants and Cafés**: Various dining options, including local and international cuisines.
  - ■ **Shopping**: Small selection of shops offering souvenirs, books, and travel essentials.
  - ■ **Public Transport Accessibility**: Easy access to buses, taxis, and ride-sharing services.
- ○ **Website**: Aeroparque Airport

Flights to Buenos Aires: Airlines and Routes

Buenos Aires is well-connected to major cities worldwide, with numerous airlines offering direct flights from North America, Europe, and other South American countries.

International Airlines Serving Buenos Aires

- **From North America**:
  - ○ **American Airlines**: Direct flights from **Miami (MIA)**, **Dallas (DFW)**, and **New York (JFK)**.
  - ○ **United Airlines**: Offers routes from **Houston (IAH)**.
  - ○ **Delta Airlines**: Connects from **Atlanta (ATL)**.
  - ○ **Aeromexico**: Operates flights from **Mexico City (MEX)**.
- **From Europe**:
  - ○ **British Airways**: Direct flights from **London Heathrow (LHR)**.
  - ○ **Iberia** and **Air Europa**: Flights from **Madrid (MAD)**.
  - ○ **Lufthansa**: Connects via **Frankfurt (FRA)**.
  - ○ **Air France**: Operates from **Paris Charles de Gaulle (CDG)**.
  - ○ **Alitalia**: Flies from **Rome (FCO)**.
- **From South America**:
  - ○ **LATAM Airlines**: Extensive routes from **Santiago (SCL)**, **Sao Paulo (GRU)**, and other regional hubs.
  - ○ **Gol Linhas Aéreas**: Flights from **Brazilian cities** such as **Sao Paulo**, **Rio de Janeiro**, and **Brasilia**.
  - ○ **Avianca**: Offers connections from **Bogotá (BOG)**.
  - ○ **Sky Airline**: Flies from **Chile** and **Peru**.

Domestic Airlines and Routes

- **Aerolineas Argentinas**: The national carrier offers flights from various cities across Argentina, including **Mendoza**, **Cordoba**, **Bariloche**, **Salta**, and **Ushuaia**.
- **Flybondi** and **Jetsmart**: Budget airlines that connect Buenos Aires to numerous domestic destinations, offering more affordable options for travelers.

Pricing

- **International Flights**: Round-trip tickets to Buenos Aires typically range from $800 to $1,500 USD from North America, and around $900 to $1,600 USD from Europe, depending on the season and demand.
- **Domestic Flights**: Domestic fares can range from $50 to $300 USD for one-way tickets, depending on the destination and airline.

Arrival Tips and Airport Transportation

Once you've arrived in Buenos Aires, navigating from the airport to your destination in the city is straightforward, thanks to various transportation options.

1. Transportation from Ezeiza Airport (EZE)

- **Taxi**: Official taxis are available outside the terminal. A ride to the city center typically costs around **ARS 5,000-7,000** (approximately **$14-$20 USD**). It is advisable to use the official **Taxi Ezeiza** service to avoid scams.
- **Ride-Sharing Services**: **Uber**, **Cabify**, and **Didi** operate in Buenos Aires, providing a convenient and sometimes cheaper alternative to taxis.
- **Shuttle Services**: The **Tienda León** shuttle offers comfortable bus transfers to the downtown area (Retiro station), costing around **ARS 3,000** (about **$8 USD**). Private cars and vans are also available for a higher price.
- **Public Bus (Colectivo)**: For budget travelers, bus **line 8** runs from Ezeiza to the city center, costing just **ARS 50-100** (less than **$1 USD**). However, the journey can take up to 2 hours and may not be ideal if you have a lot of luggage.

2. Transportation from Aeroparque (AEP)

- **Taxi or Ride-Share**: The short distance to the city center means a taxi ride typically costs **ARS 2,000-3,000** (about **$6-$10 USD**). Ride-sharing services are also readily available.
- **Bus Services**: Several public buses (e.g., lines **33**, **37**, **45**, **160**) connect the airport to different parts of the city, with fares around **ARS 50-80**.

- **Suburban Train**: The **Belgrano Norte Line** has a nearby station (**Scalabrini Ortiz**) that connects to the city's rail network, ideal for accessing the northern suburbs.

Ferry and Bus Options from Neighboring Countries

For those traveling from neighboring countries, Buenos Aires is accessible by both ferry and bus, offering scenic alternatives to flying.

Ferry Services from Uruguay

- **Buquebus**: The most popular ferry service between Buenos Aires and **Montevideo** or **Colonia del Sacramento** in Uruguay. The ferry from **Montevideo** takes about **2 hours 15 minutes**, while the trip from **Colonia** takes **1 hour**.
  - **Pricing**: One-way tickets range from **$60 to $150 USD**, depending on the route and seating class.
  - **Facilities**: Onboard amenities include a duty-free shop, café, and comfortable seating.
  - **Website**: https://www.buquebus.com
- **Colonia Express**: Offers an affordable alternative for traveling from **Colonia del Sacramento** to Buenos Aires.
  - **Pricing**: Tickets start at around **$40 USD** one-way.
  - **Travel Time**: Approximately **1 hour**.
  - **Website**: https://www.coloniaexpress.com

Long-Distance Buses

Bus travel is a common and affordable way to get to Buenos Aires from other South American countries, including **Brazil**, **Chile**, **Paraguay**, and **Bolivia**.

- **Bus Terminals**: The main terminal for long-distance buses in Buenos Aires is **Terminal de Omnibus Retiro**, located near the city center.
- **Popular Bus Companies**:
  - **Andesmar**: Connects Buenos Aires to **Mendoza**, **Cordoba**, and Chilean cities like **Santiago**.

- ○ **Crucero del Norte**: Routes from **Brazil**, **Paraguay**, and northern Argentina.
- ○ **Flecha Bus**: Serves destinations across Argentina and Uruguay.
- • **Pricing and Travel Times**:
  - ○ **From Santiago, Chile: 14-18 hours**, costing around **$70-$120 USD**.
  - ○ **From Sao Paulo, Brazil: 30-36 hours**, with prices ranging from **$150-$250 USD**.
  - ○ **From Asunción, Paraguay: 18-20 hours**, costing approximately **$60-$100 USD**.

Tips for Bus Travel

- • **Comfort Classes**: Many long-distance buses in Argentina offer **different classes of seating**: **Cama** (reclining seats), **Semi-Cama** (partially reclining seats), and **Ejecutivo** (luxury seating).
- • **Booking in Advance**: It is advisable to book tickets in advance during peak travel seasons (summer and major holidays) to secure the best seats and prices.
- • **Safety Precautions**: Choose reputable bus companies for safety and comfort, especially for overnight trips.

Chapter 4: Getting Around Buenos Aires

Buenos Aires, with its blend of European architecture and Latin American flair, is a sprawling city that offers a variety of transportation options to explore its diverse neighborhoods. Whether you're navigating the vibrant streets of Palermo, strolling through the historic avenues of San Telmo, or heading to the Recoleta Cemetery, understanding the city's transportation network can make your visit smoother and more enjoyable. In this chapter, we'll cover the main methods for getting around, including public transportation, taxis, ride-sharing, biking, walking, and essential travel apps.

Public Transportation: Subte (Metro), Buses, and Trains

Buenos Aires has an extensive public transportation system that is both affordable and convenient for tourists. The primary modes include the Subte (metro), buses (colectivos), and commuter trains. Here's a detailed look at each option:

1. Subte (Metro)

The Subte, Buenos Aires' metro system, is one of the oldest in Latin America and a popular way to get around the city. It consists of six lines (A, B, C, D, E, and H), covering key areas, including downtown, Palermo, Recoleta, and other central neighborhoods.

- **Operating Hours**: The Subte operates from around 5:30 AM to 11:30 PM (Mon-Sat) and 8:00 AM to 10:30 PM (Sundays and holidays).
- **Fares**: A single journey costs approximately ARS 70 (around $0.20 USD), and fares decrease slightly with frequent use. Tickets can be purchased via the SUBE card, a rechargeable contactless card that works across all forms of public transportation.
- **Tips**:
    - Avoid rush hours (8-10 AM and 6-8 PM) when trains can get crowded.
    - The Subte stations often feature murals and art displays, adding a cultural experience to your commute.

2. Buses (Colectivos)

The city's buses, known as colectivos, cover an extensive network of over 200 routes, making it possible to reach virtually any part of Buenos Aires. Buses run 24 hours a day, though frequency decreases at night.

- **Fares**: The fare starts at ARS 50 (around $0.15 USD) and is based on the distance traveled. Payment is made using the SUBE card, which can be purchased and recharged at kiosks, Subte stations, and some convenience stores.

- **Popular Routes for Tourists**:
  - **Bus 29**: Connects Palermo, Recoleta, and San Telmo, passing many tourist attractions.

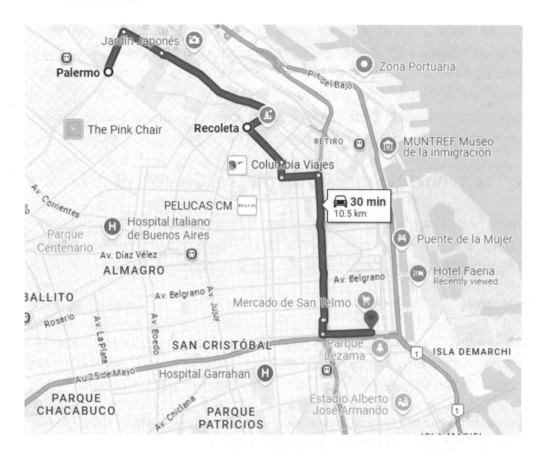

  - **Bus 64**: Travels between the Retiro bus station and the Belgrano neighborhood, offering views of several city landmarks.

- **Tips**:
  - You need to tell the driver your destination upon boarding so they can set the correct fare.
  - Colectivos don't provide change, so make sure your SUBE card is loaded with sufficient credit.

3. Trains

Buenos Aires' commuter train network connects the city with suburban areas and some nearby provinces, such as Tigre and La Plata. While less relevant for navigating central Buenos Aires, trains are ideal for day trips.

- **Popular Lines**:
  - **Tigre Line (Mitre Railway)**: A scenic ride from Retiro to the town of Tigre, known for its river delta and water activities.

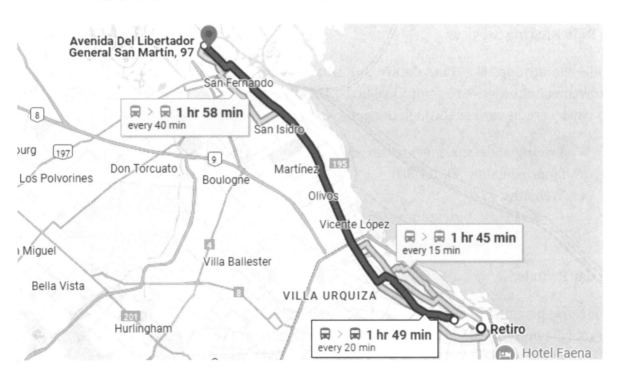

  - **La Plata Line (Roca Railway)**: Connects the city with La Plata, the capital of Buenos Aires Province.
- **Fares**: Starting from ARS 25 (about $0.07 USD), depending on the line and destination. Payment is made with the SUBE card.

Taxi, Ride-Sharing, and Car Rentals

Buenos Aires offers multiple options for on-demand transportation, including traditional taxis, ride-sharing services, and car rentals.

1. Taxis

Taxis are widely available and can be hailed on the street, ordered via phone, or through mobile apps like BA Taxi, which is operated by the city government.

- **Pricing**: Taxi fares start with a base rate of ARS 300 (about $0.85 USD) plus ARS 30 (around $0.09 USD) for each 200 meters. Fares increase by 20% after 10 PM.
- **Safety Tips**:
    - Use official black-and-yellow taxis with a visible license number.
    - Always ask for the meter to be turned on ("por favor, ponga el taxímetro").

2. Ride-Sharing Services

Ride-sharing apps like **Uber**, **Cabify**, and **DiDi** operate in Buenos Aires and offer a convenient alternative to traditional taxis. These services are often cheaper and allow you to pay by credit card or through the app, avoiding the need for cash.

- **Pricing**: Ride-sharing fares are dynamic but generally start at around ARS 250 (approximately $0.70 USD).
- **Websites**:
    - https://www.uber.com
    - https://www.cabify.com

3. Car Rentals

For those planning to explore areas outside the city or take day trips, renting a car can be a practical option. Several car rental companies, including **Avis**, **Hertz**, and **Localiza**, have offices at Ezeiza International Airport and various locations throughout the city.

- **Pricing**: Daily rentals start at around ARS 10,000 (approximately $28 USD) for a compact car.
- **Driving Tips**:
    - Traffic can be heavy in central Buenos Aires, especially during peak hours.
    - Parking is scarce in busy neighborhoods, and parking garages can be expensive (around ARS 1,000 per hour or $2.85 USD).

Biking and Walking in the City

Buenos Aires is an increasingly bike-friendly city, with over 250 kilometers of dedicated bike lanes and a popular public bike-sharing program. Walking is also a great way to explore the city's parks, plazas, and neighborhoods.

1. Biking

The city's bike-sharing program, **EcoBici**, offers free bicycles for use in the city. It is a great option for tourists who want to explore areas like Palermo, Puerto Madero, and the Costanera Norte.

- **EcoBici Program**:
    - **Cost**: Free for the first hour (Mon-Fri) and first two hours (weekends). After that, additional charges apply.
    - **Requirements**: Registration via the EcoBici app is required, and a valid ID must be provided.
    - **Website**: EcoBici
- **Bike Tours**: Several companies offer guided bike tours, such as **Biking Buenos Aires**, which provides half-day and full-day tours, including visits to famous landmarks and neighborhoods.
    - **Pricing**: Tours start at around $35 USD for a half-day tour.
    - **Website**: https://www.bikingbuenosaires.com

2. Walking

Buenos Aires' layout makes walking a delightful way to explore the city. Key areas for walking tours include:

- **Recoleta and Retiro**: Walk through elegant streets lined with historic buildings and parks.
- **San Telmo**: Explore cobblestone streets, antique shops, and street markets.
- **Palermo**: Wander through parks and trendy neighborhoods filled with cafes and boutiques.
- **Walking Tips**:
    - Wear comfortable shoes, as some streets are uneven.
    - Watch out for traffic at intersections, even where pedestrian signals are present.

Navigating Buenos Aires with Mobile Apps

Using the right apps can make getting around Buenos Aires much more manageable. Here are some essential apps for travelers:

1. Moovit: An excellent app for navigating the city's public transport system, offering real-time information on buses, Subte, and trains.

- **Website**: https://www.moovitapp.com

2. BA Cómo Llego: A local app designed specifically for Buenos Aires that provides route options for walking, biking, driving, and public transit.

3. EcoBici App: The official app for the city's bike-sharing program, allowing users to locate and rent bikes.

4. Google Maps: Offers detailed navigation for walking, driving, and public transport, including accurate schedules for the Subte and buses.

5. BA Taxi: The official taxi app, connecting users with licensed taxis for safer rides.

Tips for Avoiding Traffic and Getting Around Efficiently

Buenos Aires can be a bustling city, especially during peak times. Here are some strategies to navigate the city efficiently:

1. Use the Subte During Peak Hours: The Subte is often the fastest option during rush hours (8-10 AM and 6-8 PM), as it avoids traffic jams.

2. Avoid Major Streets During High Traffic Times: Streets like Avenida 9 de Julio and Corrientes can be heavily congested. Use side streets or the city's bike lanes.

3. Take Advantage of Biking for Short Distances: Cycling is often faster than driving or taking a taxi for short distances due to traffic and parking limitations.

4. Plan Routes in Advance Using Apps: Check real-time traffic data and public transit schedules to avoid delays.

Chapter 5: Neighborhoods of Buenos Aires

Buenos Aires is a city of diverse neighborhoods, each with its unique character and charm. From historical districts filled with tango and antiques to modern areas boasting sleek architecture and luxury, the city's barrios offer a rich tapestry of experiences. In this chapter, we explore the most iconic neighborhoods, each with must-visit attractions, tips for what to see and do, pricing information, and helpful resources to enhance your travel experience.

Microcentro: The Heart of the City

People Walking on Pedestrian Street in Microcentro

The Microcentro is Buenos Aires' bustling downtown district, where historical landmarks and modern business hubs meet. The area is known for its cultural, political, and financial significance, and is home to many of the city's top attractions.

Highlights

- **Plaza de Mayo**: The city's central square has been a focal point of political activity for centuries. It is surrounded by historic buildings such as the **Casa Rosada** (the Presidential Palace), where visitors can take guided tours to learn about Argentina's political history.
    - **Location**: Balcarce 50, C1064 CABA, Argentina
    - **Pricing**: Free to enter the plaza; Casa Rosada tours are free, but reservations are required.

- **Website**: https://www.casarosada.gob.ar
- **Teatro Colón**: A world-renowned opera house and a masterpiece of architecture, the Teatro Colón offers guided tours that provide a glimpse into its lavish interior and historical significance. Attending a performance is a must for classical music enthusiasts.

  - **Location**: Cerrito 628, C1010 CABA, Argentina
  - **Pricing**: Guided tours cost approximately $10 USD; performance tickets range from $15 to $200 USD.
  - **Website**: https://www.teatrocolon.org.ar

- **Florida Street**: A pedestrian shopping street lined with boutiques, street vendors, and cafes, Florida Street is perfect for souvenir hunting and people-watching.

Things to Do

- Take a walking tour of **Avenida de Mayo**, known for its architectural gems, including the **Palacio Barolo**, which offers panoramic views of the city.
- Enjoy a coffee at the iconic **Café Tortoni**, one of the city's oldest cafes, established in 1858.

San Telmo: Tango, Antiques, and History

San Telma

San Telmo is one of Buenos Aires' oldest neighborhoods, known for its cobblestone streets, colonial architecture, and bohemian atmosphere. The area is rich in history and culture, offering a glimpse into the city's past while being a center for tango music and dance.

Crowds at San Telmo Traditional Market

Highlights

- **San Telmo Market**: Established in 1897, this indoor market is famous for its antique shops, local food vendors, and eclectic stalls selling everything from vintage clothing to fresh produce.
  - **Location**: Defensa 961, C1065 AAU, Buenos Aires, Argentina
  - **Pricing**: Free to enter; prices for antiques and food vary.
  - **Website**: https://mercadodesantelmo.com.ar
- **Plaza Dorrego**: On Sundays, Plaza Dorrego hosts an antiques fair where you can find unique souvenirs and enjoy live tango performances.
  - **Location**: Humberto 1º 400, C1103 CABA, Argentina
  - **Pricing**: Free to attend the market and performances.
- **El Zanjón de Granados**: An underground labyrinth of tunnels dating back to the 16th century, El Zanjón offers guided tours that delve into the city's early history.
  - **Location**: Defensa 755, C1065 AAO, Buenos Aires, Argentina
  - **Pricing**: Approximately $15 USD for a guided tour.
  - **Website**: http://www.elzanjon.com.ar

Things to Do

- **Tango Shows and Milongas**: Attend a tango show or participate in a milonga (tango dance event) to experience the essence of San Telmo.
- Explore the neighborhood's **street art**, which adds a vibrant touch to its historic atmosphere.

La Boca: Colorful Streets and Soccer Passion

Colourful Building in Caminito Street

La Boca is a vibrant neighborhood famous for its colorful houses, street art, and deep-rooted soccer culture. The area was historically settled by Italian immigrants, which influences its unique character.

Highlights

- **Caminito**: This open-air museum street is the heart of La Boca, filled with brightly painted buildings, tango dancers, and street artists. It's the perfect place to immerse yourself in the neighborhood's lively atmosphere.
    - **Location**: Caminito, C1169 CABA, Buenos Aires, Argentina

- **Pricing**: Free to walk around; street performances may ask for tips.
- **La Bombonera**: Home to the famous Boca Juniors football club, this stadium is a must-visit for soccer fans. Tours of the stadium and museum provide insights into the club's storied history.
    - **Location**: Brandsen 805, C1161 CABA, Buenos Aires, Argentina
    - **Pricing**: Stadium tours and museum tickets cost around $15 USD.
    - **Website**: https://www.bocajuniors.com.ar/el-club/la-bombonera

Things to Do

- **Watch a Boca Juniors game** if the season is in full swing, or catch a local tango show in one of the many bars around Caminito.
- **Visit Fundación PROA**, a contemporary art museum offering changing exhibitions in a renovated historical building.

Palermo: Parks, Cafés, and Nightlife

Palermo is the largest barrio in Buenos Aires, known for its green spaces, vibrant nightlife, and trendy cafes. The area is divided into sub-neighborhoods, including Palermo Soho and Palermo Hollywood, each with its unique appeal.

Highlights

- **Bosques de Palermo (Palermo Woods)**: This large urban park features lakes, rose gardens, and walking trails, making it a favorite spot for locals and tourists alike.
    - **Location**: Av. Infanta Isabel 410, C1425 CABA, Buenos Aires, Argentina

- **Pricing**: Free entry.
- **Jardín Japonés (Japanese Garden)**: The Japanese Garden is a peaceful oasis in the city, featuring traditional Japanese landscaping, koi ponds, and a tea house.
    - **Location**: Av. Casares 2966, C1425 CABA, Buenos Aires, Argentina
    - **Pricing**: Entrance fee is about $4 USD.
    - **Website**: https://www.jardinjapones.org.ar
- **Palermo Soho**: A hub for shopping, dining, and nightlife, Palermo Soho is famous for its boutique stores, street art, and laid-back vibe.
    - **Things to Do**: Visit local designer boutiques, enjoy a drink at a rooftop bar, and explore the area's murals.

Nightlife

- Palermo's nightlife is legendary, with bars, clubs, and music venues that stay open until dawn. **Niceto Club** is a popular spot for live music and dancing.
    - **Website**: https://www.nicetoclub.com

Recoleta: Elegance, Cemeteries, and Cultural Gems

Recoleta is a sophisticated neighborhood known for its European-style architecture, cultural institutions, and historic cemetery. It offers a mix of luxury and history, appealing to those looking for a refined experience.

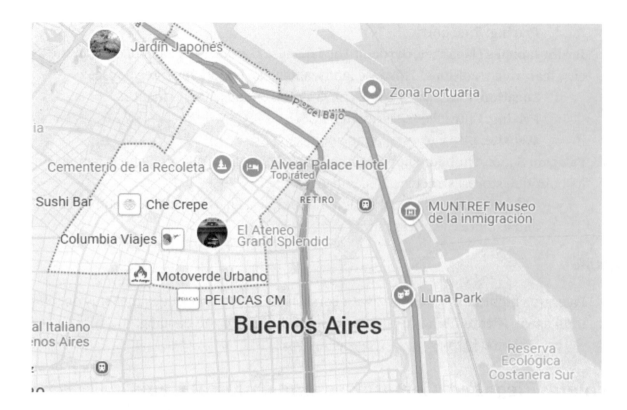

Highlights

- **Recoleta Cemetery**: Famous for its elaborate tombs and mausoleums, Recoleta Cemetery is the final resting place of many notable figures, including Eva Perón. It's one of the world's most famous cemeteries and a fascinating place to explore.

  - **Location**: Junín 1760, C1113 CABA, Buenos Aires, Argentina
  - **Pricing**: Free entry; guided tours available for around $10 USD.
- **Museo Nacional de Bellas Artes (MNBA)**: This art museum houses an extensive collection of Argentine and European art, making it a top cultural destination in Buenos Aires.

- **Location**: Av. del Libertador 1473, C1425 CABA, Buenos Aires, Argentina
- **Pricing**: Free entry.
- **Website**: https://www.bellasartes.gob.ar
- **El Ateneo Grand Splendid**: A former theater turned bookstore, El Ateneo is considered one of the most beautiful bookstores in the world.
    - **Location**: Av. Santa Fe 1860, C1123 CABA, Buenos Aires, Argentina
    - **Pricing**: Free to enter.

Puerto Madero: Waterfront Dining and Modern Architecture

Puerto Madero is the city's newest and most modern district, offering a mix of high-rise buildings, luxurious hotels, and waterfront dining. The area was once an old port and has been revitalized into a prime urban spot.

Highlights

- **Puente de la Mujer (Women's Bridge)**: This iconic pedestrian bridge symbolizes the modern transformation of Puerto Madero. It's a great spot for photography, especially at sunset.
  - **Location**: Dock 3, Puerto Madero, Buenos Aires, Argentina
  - **Pricing**: Free to visit.
- **Reserva Ecológica Costanera Sur**: An ecological reserve on the edge of the city, offering trails for walking, cycling, and birdwatching.
  - **Location**: Av. Tristán Achával Rodríguez 1550, C1107 CABA, Buenos Aires, Argentina
  - **Pricing**: Free entry.
- **Dining and Nightlife**: Puerto Madero is known for upscale dining, including renowned steakhouses such as **Cabaña Las Lilas** and seafood restaurants like **La Parolaccia**.
  - **Website**: https://www.laslilas.com, https://www.laparolaccia.com

Belgrano and Núñez: Residential Charm and Local Vibes

Belgrano and Núñez are primarily residential neighborhoods, offering a glimpse into the local way of life. These areas are characterized by tree-lined streets, historic houses, and laid-back atmospheres.

Highlights

- **Barrancas de Belgrano**: A park designed by the same landscape architect who planned Buenos Aires' parks, Barrancas de Belgrano is ideal for leisurely walks and weekend markets.
  - **Location**: 11 de Septiembre 1900, Buenos Aires, Argentina
  - **Pricing**: Free to visit.
- **Chinatown (Barrio Chino)**: Buenos Aires' Chinatown is a lively area full of Asian restaurants, shops, and cultural events.
  - **Location**: Arribeños 2100, Buenos Aires, Argentina

Things to Do

- Stroll through **Avenida Cabildo**, known for its shopping and local cafes.
- Visit **River Plate Stadium**, home to one of Argentina's biggest soccer clubs.

Villa Crespo and Almagro: Hipster Hangouts and Local Flavors

Villa Crespo and Almagro are up-and-coming neighborhoods with a mix of traditional and modern vibes. Known for their hipster culture, boutique stores, and bohemian cafes, these barrios are perfect for those seeking an authentic local experience.

Highlights

- **Mercado de Villa Crespo**: A contemporary food market offering local dishes and gourmet treats.
    - **Location**: Thames 747, Villa Crespo, Buenos Aires, Argentina
    - **Pricing**: Prices vary depending on the vendor.
- **Parque Centenario**: A popular park in Almagro known for its weekend craft markets, outdoor concerts, and recreational areas.
    - **Location**: Av. Patricias Argentinas 270, C1405 CABA, Buenos Aires, Argentina
    - **Pricing**: Free entry.

Things to Do

- Experience the nightlife at **La Catedral Club**, a popular tango venue in Almagro.
    - **Website**: https://www.lacatedralclub.com

Chapter 6: Top Attractions in Buenos Aires

Buenos Aires is a city full of history, culture, and lively streets. Its top attractions include everything from historic sites to modern art museums, giving visitors a range of things to see and do. Below is a simpler description of these must-visit places, including where they are, what to expect, costs, and helpful links.

Plaza de Mayo and Casa Rosada

People Walking at Plaza de Mayo

Casa Rosada in Plaza de Mayo

Location: Plaza de Mayo, C1002 CABA, Buenos Aires
Website: www.casarosada.gob.ar
Entry Fee: Free to visit the square; Casa Rosada guided tours are also free but must be booked ahead.

Plaza de Mayo is the main square in Buenos Aires and a key place for Argentina's history and politics. It is surrounded by important buildings like the **Cabildo**, the **Metropolitan Cathedral**, and the **Casa Rosada**, which is the pink-colored presidential palace. The balcony of the Casa Rosada is famous because people like **Evita Perón** once spoke to crowds from there. The square is also a gathering spot for protests and celebrations.

Tours inside Casa Rosada show you places like the president's office and historic rooms. The tours are available on weekends and holidays for free, but you need to reserve a spot online.

Highlights:

- The famous **balcony of Casa Rosada**, associated with Evita Perón.
- The **May Pyramid**, a monument celebrating Argentina's independence.
- Known for hosting political events and public gatherings.

Teatro Colón: A World-Class Opera House

Location: Cerrito 628, C1010 CABA, Buenos Aires
Website: www.teatrocolon.org.ar
Entry Fee: Tours cost about 6,000 ARS ($17 USD); show ticket prices vary.

Teatro Colón is one of the most famous opera houses in the world, known for its amazing sound quality. Opened in 1908, it is a beautiful building with marble staircases, stained glass windows, and fancy sculptures. Some of the world's best musicians and singers have performed here.

You can take guided tours that show the theater's history and the effort that goes into keeping it in top condition. If you can, watching a performance like an opera, ballet, or concert is a memorable experience.

Highlights:

- The grand **Main Hall**, with its elegant seating and chandeliers.
- The **Golden Hall**, which is decorated with gold and beautiful paintings.
- A place where famous performers like **Luciano Pavarotti** have sung.

El Caminito: The Iconic Street in La Boca

Location: Caminito, C1161AAE, Buenos Aires
Entry Fee: Free to visit (some activities may cost extra).

El Caminito is a famous street in the colorful **La Boca** area. The neighborhood is known for its lively art and tango dancing. The buildings are painted in bright colors, reflecting the area's immigrant history, especially from Italy. There are street performers, artists selling their work, and many small shops.

Even though it is a popular tourist spot, El Caminito still feels authentic, showcasing local art and tango culture. You can also find restaurants serving traditional Argentine dishes like **asado** (grilled meat) and **choripán** (sausage sandwich).

Highlights:

- The colorful houses, called **conventillos**, which now house art studios and shops.
- **Live street performances**, including tango dancers.
- Local food stands and restaurants offering Argentine dishes.

Recoleta Cemetery: Graves of the Famous and Infamous

Location: Junín 1760, C1113 CABA, Buenos Aires
Website: turismo.buenosaires.gob.ar
Entry Fee: Free entry; guided tours cost 2,000-3,000 ARS ($5-9 USD).

The **Recoleta Cemetery** is a unique and famous place in Buenos Aires, known for its fancy marble graves and sculptures. Many important people from Argentina's history are buried here, including **Eva Perón (Evita)**. The cemetery's layout is like a maze, and each tomb tells a story about the country's past and its notable families.

When visiting, you can find the graves of presidents, military leaders, writers, and even a descendant of Napoleon. It's more than just a cemetery; it's a place where history and architecture come together.

Highlights:

- **Evita's Tomb**, which attracts many visitors.
- The **beautiful architecture** of the graves, with styles like Art Nouveau and Gothic.
- Guided tours that explain the lives of the people buried there.

Museo Nacional de Bellas Artes (MNBA)

Location: Av. del Libertador 1473, CABA, Buenos Aires
Website: www.bellasartes.gob.ar
Entry Fee: Free for the main exhibits; some temporary shows may charge.

The **Museo Nacional de Bellas Artes** is Argentina's top art museum, featuring one of the biggest art collections in Latin America. The museum has works from famous European artists like **Monet, Degas, Goya**, and **Rembrandt**, as well as pieces by well-known Argentine artists. You'll find paintings, sculptures, and decorative arts from different time periods.

The museum often hosts special events, such as film screenings and cultural programs, making it a lively place to visit.

Highlights:

- A large collection of **Argentine art**, showing the country's culture over time.
- **European masterpieces** from different art movements, such as Impressionism.
- **Free admission**, making it a great budget-friendly option.

Palermo's Bosques and Japanese Garden

Location: Av. Infanta Isabel 410, C1425 CABA, Buenos Aires

Street View

Website: www.jardinjapones.org.ar

Entry Fee: Free for Palermo's Bosques; the Japanese Garden costs about 1,500 ARS ($4 USD).

Bosques de Palermo is the city's biggest park, featuring over 1,000 acres of gardens, lakes, and paths. It's popular for picnicking, jogging, boating, and cycling. Inside the park is the **Japanese Garden**, which is full of koi ponds, bridges, and a tea house, offering a peaceful place to relax.

The Japanese Garden is one of the largest outside Japan and provides a quiet space away from the busy city. It's great for a walk, meditation, or photography.

Highlights:

- **El Rosedal**, a rose garden with thousands of flowers and a lake.
- The peaceful setting of the **Japanese Garden**, with traditional ponds and plants.
- Activities like **boat rentals** and **bike riding**.

MALBA (Museum of Latin American Art)

MALBA

Location: Av. Pres. Figueroa Alcorta 3415, C1425 CABA, Buenos Aires
Website: www.malba.org.ar
Entry Fee: Around 2,500 ARS ($7 USD); discounts available.

The **Museum of Latin American Art of Buenos Aires (MALBA)** displays modern and contemporary Latin American art. The collection includes famous pieces by artists such as **Frida Kahlo, Diego Rivera,** and **Tarsila do Amaral**. There are also temporary exhibitions, film events, and cultural activities, making it an exciting place to visit.

The museum mainly showcases 20th and 21st-century art, focusing on social and political themes, as well as abstract and modern styles.

Highlights:

- **"Self-Portrait with Monkey" by Frida Kahlo**, a popular artwork at the museum.
- **Changing exhibitions** featuring up-and-coming Latin American artists.
- **Film screenings** and cultural events linked to the exhibitions.

Buenos Aires Ecological Reserve

Location: Av. Dr. Tristán Achával Rodríguez 1550, CABA, Buenos Aires
Website: www.buenosaires.gob.ar/areas/med_ambiente/reserva_ecologica
Entry Fee: Free.

The **Buenos Aires Ecological Reserve** is a large natural area near **Puerto Madero**, offering a break from the city. The reserve has over 860 acres of grasslands, wetlands, and forests, with many walking and biking trails. It's a great place for birdwatching, jogging, or just enjoying the outdoors.

The reserve offers beautiful views of the **Río de la Plata** and the city's skyline, making it an ideal spot for nature lovers.

Highlights:

- **Birdwatching**, with over 200 species of birds, including ducks and herons.
- **Paths for walking and biking** through different environments.
- Scenic views of the river and the city.

Chapter 7: Cultural Experiences

Buenos Aires is a city full of life and rich culture, blending European charm with Latin American energy. It's a place where traditions like dance, food, art, and sports bring the city to life. In this chapter, you'll learn about cultural experiences that give Buenos Aires its unique character, including tango, soccer, local foods, and colorful murals.

Tango Shows and Milongas: Where to Dance and Watch

Tango, often called "the soul of Buenos Aires," began in the city's poorer neighborhoods in the late 1800s. It's more than just a dance—it's a way of expressing deep emotions and telling the story of Argentina. There are many ways to experience tango in Buenos Aires, from watching professional shows to dancing at local tango halls (called milongas) or even taking a class.

- **Top Tango Shows**:
    - **El Querandí** (San Telmo, Peru 302, $70-$100 for dinner and show)
      One of the oldest places for tango, offering an authentic experience with a three-course meal of traditional Argentine food.
        - **Website**: https://www.querandi.com.ar
    - **Café de los Angelitos** (Balvanera, Rivadavia 2100, $100-$150 for dinner and show)
      A historic spot where famous tango musicians once performed, featuring live music and dancers.
        - **Website**: https://www.cafedelosangelitos.com
    - **Rojo Tango** (Puerto Madero, Martha Salotti 445, $200-$300 for dinner and show)
      A high-end tango show in the stylish Faena Hotel, offering a glamorous performance with dramatic lighting and fancy costumes.
        - **Website**: https://www.rojotango.com
- **Popular Milongas**:
    - **La Catedral Club** (Almagro, Sarmiento 4006, $5-$10 entrance fee)
      A relaxed, artistic space with an informal vibe, great for beginners who want to take a tango lesson.
    - **Salon Canning** (Palermo, Scalabrini Ortiz 1331, $10-$15 entrance fee)
      A more traditional tango hall where you can watch skilled dancers and enjoy live music.

- **El Beso** (Balvanera, Riobamba 416, $8-$12 entrance fee)
  A cozy, classic place where both locals and visitors come to dance and learn about traditional tango rules.

The Buenos Aires Food Scene: Traditional Dishes and Trends

Buenos Aires is a food lover's dream, with a mix of traditional dishes, new food trends, and a love for meat that's central to the culture. Different neighborhoods bring their own flavors, from Italian-inspired pastas to tasty street food.

- **Must-Try Traditional Dishes**:
  - **Asado**:

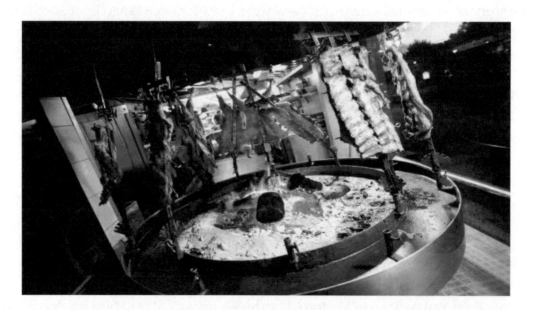

Asado

  - Argentine barbecue, where meat is slow-cooked over wood or charcoal. It's a popular experience and often served with chimichurri sauce and grilled veggies. Try it at **Parrilla Don Julio** (Palermo, Guatemala 4691, $25-$50 per person).
    - **Website**: https://www.parrilladonjulio.com

- Empanadas:

  - Small pastries filled with meat, cheese, or vegetables. They're popular as snacks and can be found all over the city. A good place to try them is **La Cocina** (Recoleta, Pueyrredón 1508, $1.50-$2.50 each).
  - **Milanesa**: A breaded and fried meat cutlet, like a schnitzel, usually served with fries. You can find many versions at **El Club de la Milanesa** (multiple locations, $10-$20 per dish).
    - **Website**: https://www.elclubdelamilanesa.com
- **New Food Trends**:
  - **Gourmet Street Food**: Food trucks and vendors are offering upgraded versions of street food, like fusion tacos and artisanal hot dogs.
  - **Plant-Based Dining**: More vegetarian and vegan options are popping up, like **Sacro** (Palermo, Costa Rica 6038, $20-$40 per person), which serves creative plant-based dishes.
    - **Website**: https://www.sacro.com.ar
  - **Craft Beer**: The local craft beer scene is growing, with many breweries offering tastings. **Buller Brewing Company** (Recoleta, Junín 1747, $3-$5 per pint) is a popular spot for locally brewed beers.
    - **Website**: https://www.bullerbrewing.com

Mate Culture: Drinking Like a Local

Mate, a traditional herbal tea made from the yerba mate plant, is more than just a drink in Argentina—it's a social ritual. People share mate as a sign of friendship and connection. The tea is prepared in a hollowed-out gourd and drunk through a metal straw called a bombilla.

- **How to Drink Mate**:
    - Fill the gourd halfway with yerba mate.
    - Tilt the gourd so the leaves are at an angle.
    - Insert the bombilla (metal straw) into the lower side.
    - Pour hot (but not boiling) water over the yerba and sip.
- **Where to Experience Mate**:
    - **El Gato Negro** (San Nicolás, Av. Corrientes 1669)
      A historic shop where you can buy yerba mate and learn how to prepare it.
    - **Mate & Co. Workshops** (Palermo, various pop-up locations)
      Offers workshops on how to prepare and drink mate, as well as the cultural history behind it.

The Passion of Soccer: Stadium Tours and Match Experiences

Soccer (fútbol) is a huge part of life in Argentina, and Buenos Aires is home to some of the country's most famous teams, like **Boca Juniors** and **River Plate**. Watching a soccer game in Buenos Aires is an exciting experience filled with energy, loud chants, and waving flags.

- **Stadiums to Visit**:
    - **La Bombonera (Estadio Alberto J. Armando)**

    - Location: La Boca, Brandsen 805, Tours: $20, Match tickets: $50-$150.
    - Home to Boca Juniors, known for its steep stands and lively crowd. Tours include the museum and trophy room.

- **Website**: https://www.bocajuniors.com.ar
  - **El Monumental (Estadio Monumental Antonio Vespucio Liberti)**

- Location: Núñez, Av. Pres. Figueroa Alcorta 7597, Tours: $20, Match tickets: $50-$200.
- The largest stadium in Argentina, home to River Plate, and famous for hosting big matches. The tour covers the stadium and the River Plate Museum.
- **Website**: https://www.cariverplate.com.ar
- **Match Day Advice**:
  - **Get Tickets Early**: Games can sell out fast, especially big matches like Boca vs. River. Buy from the official club websites or soccer tour agencies.
  - **Be Safe**: Avoid wearing rival team colors in certain areas and follow local advice.

Festivals and Events: Carnival, Book Fair, and More

Buenos Aires is a city of festivals, with events all year round that celebrate its culture. Whether it's lively parades or book fairs, there's always something going on.

- **Popular Festivals**:
  - **Carnaval Porteño** (February)

- Celebrated with parades, drumming, and dancing in the streets. Different neighborhoods have carnival groups that perform traditional music and dance.
  - **Feria Internacional del Libro** (April-May)
    - The International Book Fair is a major event attracting writers and readers from around the world, held at **La Rural Exhibition Center** in Palermo.
    - **Website**: https://www.el-libro.org.ar
  - **BAFICI (Buenos Aires International Festival of Independent Cinema)** (April)
    - Features independent films from Argentina and other countries, with screenings and workshops across the city.

Street Art and Murals: Exploring the Urban Canvas

Buenos Aires is famous for its street art, with colorful murals and graffiti covering many city walls. These artworks often tell stories about social issues, politics, and everyday life, blending art with the city's culture.

- **Best Areas for Street Art**:
  - **Palermo**: Known for its trendy atmosphere, with many murals by popular artists. Stroll along Gorriti or Honduras streets to see some of the best pieces.
  - **La Boca**: Famous for the brightly colored buildings along El Caminito, with street art reflecting the area's immigrant history and soccer culture.
  - **Barracas**: Home to some of the biggest murals in the city, including works by well-known street artist Alfredo Segatori.
- **Street Art Tours**:
  - **Graffiti Mundo** (Tours from $25, Locations: Palermo and nearby areas) Offers guided tours that explain the history of street art in Buenos Aires and highlight key artists and murals.
    - **Website**: https://www.graffitimundo.com
- **Exploring On Your Own**:
  - Use a street art map app or follow local Instagram accounts to find popular murals.
  - Remember to respect private property and only explore during the day.

Chapter 8: Buenos Aires for Food Lovers

Buenos Aires is a great place for food enthusiasts, offering a mix of traditional Argentine dishes, modern cuisine, and international flavors. The city's food culture combines European heritage with local ingredients, making it perfect for both locals and tourists. This chapter will guide you through the city's must-try foods, fine dining options, coffee spots, markets, and wine tastings.

Traditional Foods: Grilled Meats, Empanadas, and Sweet Treats

Argentine food is known for its grilled meats, tasty pastries, and sweet treats. Here are the must-try traditional foods:

1. **Grilled Meats (Parrillas)**
   - **Parrillas** are places where Argentina's famous meats are cooked on a grill. Popular cuts include **sirloin**, **skirt steak**, and **ribs**, usually served with a sauce called **chimichurri**.
   - **Recommended Places**:
     - **Don Julio** (Palermo): A top steakhouse known for tender steaks and a large wine selection. **Cost**: ARS 6,000 - 12,000 ($17 - $35 USD) per main dish.
     - **La Brigada** (San Telmo): Traditional grilling with a variety of meats. **Cost**: ARS 5,000 - 10,000 ($15 - $30 USD).
     - **El Pobre Luis** (Belgrano): Features a mix of Argentine and Uruguayan meats. **Cost**: ARS 4,000 - 9,000 ($12 - $26 USD).
2. **Empanadas**
   - Empanadas are savory pastries filled with different ingredients, such as beef, chicken, or cheese.
   - **Top Spots**:
     - **El Sanjuanino** (Recoleta): Known for its spicy beef empanadas. **Cost**: ARS 500 - 800 ($1.50 - $2.50 USD) each.
     - **La Cocina** (Recoleta): Offers a variety of flavors, including beef and spinach. **Cost**: ARS 400 - 700 ($1.20 - $2 USD) each.
3. **Sweet Treats (Dulce de Leche)**
   - **Dulce de leche** is a caramel-like spread made from milk and sugar, used in many desserts.
   - **Where to Try It**:

- **Freddo**: An ice cream chain famous for dulce de leche-flavored ice cream. **Cost**: ARS 2,000 - 4,000 ($6 - $12 USD).
- **La Pasticceria** (San Telmo): Offers traditional **alfajores** (cookies with dulce de leche filling). **Cost**: ARS 600 - 1,000 ($2 - $3 USD).

Fine Dining: High-End Restaurants

Buenos Aires has a growing fine dining scene, with chefs blending Argentine traditions with international styles.

Top 5 Restaurant in Buenos Aires

1. Don Julio

- **Cuisine**: Traditional Argentine Steakhouse
- **Location**: Guatemala 4699, Palermo, Buenos Aires
- **Description**: Don Julio is renowned for its high-quality, grass-fed Argentine beef cooked to perfection on a traditional parrilla (grill). The atmosphere is warm, with brick walls lined by wine bottles signed by past patrons.
- **Average Cost**: Approximately $25–$60 USD per person, with individual dishes like rib-eye or bife de chorizo around $15–$30 USD.

2. El Preferido de Palermo

- **Cuisine**: Argentine-Spanish Fusion
- **Location**: Jorge Luis Borges 2108, Palermo Soho, Buenos Aires
- **Description**: El Preferido offers a cozy, old-world vibe combined with a modern twist on traditional Spanish and Argentine dishes. Known for items like grilled octopus, empanadas, and inventive small plates.
- **Average Cost**: Around $15–$40 USD per person; small plates and tapas are about $5–$15 USD each.

3. Chila

- **Cuisine**: Fine Dining, Modern Argentine
- **Location**: Alicia Moreau de Justo 1160, Puerto Madero, Buenos Aires

- **Description**: Chila is an award-winning, high-end restaurant known for its seasonal tasting menus, featuring locally sourced ingredients and contemporary takes on Argentine cuisine. The menu is a journey through Argentina's diverse regions.
- **Average Cost**: Tasting menu prices range from $80–$150 USD per person.

4. Tegui

- **Cuisine**: Contemporary Argentine
- **Location**: Costa Rica 5852, Palermo, Buenos Aires
- **Description**: Tegui is a hidden gem with a graffiti-covered entrance leading to a sleek, sophisticated dining space. The chef's tasting menu features creative Argentine-inspired dishes with global influences, prepared with precision.
- **Average Cost**: Tasting menus run between $100–$150 USD per person.

5. Aramburu Restó

- **Cuisine**: Avant-Garde, Molecular Gastronomy
- **Location**: Salta 1050, San Telmo, Buenos Aires
- **Description**: Known for molecular gastronomy techniques, Aramburu offers a unique 12-course tasting menu that explores the boundaries of Argentine cuisine. Each dish is artfully presented, making for a memorable experience.
- **Average Cost**: $120–$160 USD per person for the tasting menu.

These restaurants vary in ambiance and price, making them standouts in Buenos Aires for both traditional and avant-garde Argentine cuisine.

Best Coffee Spots

Buenos Aires has a strong café culture, with many places to enjoy coffee and pastries.

1. **Classic Cafés**
   - **Café Tortoni** (Microcentro): A historic café famous for its atmosphere and pastries. **Cost**: Coffee and pastries for two cost ARS 2,500 - 4,000 ($7 - $12 USD).
   - **Las Violetas** (Almagro): Known for its elegant style and afternoon tea. **Cost**: ARS 4,000 - 6,000 ($12 - $18 USD).
2. **Specialty Coffee**
   - **LAB Tostadores de Café** (Palermo): A modern coffee shop for coffee lovers. **Cost**: ARS 800 - 1,500 ($2.50 - $5 USD).
   - **LATTEnTE** (Palermo): Offers high-quality coffee in a cozy setting. **Cost**: ARS 1,000 - 1,800 ($3 - $5.50 USD).

Vegetarian and Vegan Options

Even though Argentina is famous for its meat, Buenos Aires has plenty of vegetarian and vegan-friendly spots.

1. **Top Vegetarian/Vegan Places**
   - **Sacro** (Palermo): A vegan restaurant with creative dishes like plant-based sushi. **Cost**: ARS 5,000 - 9,000 ($15 - $27 USD).
   - **Hierbabuena** (San Telmo): Serves healthy vegetarian meals using organic ingredients. **Cost**: ARS 3,500 - 7,000 ($10 - $20 USD).
2. **Vegetarian Dishes at Regular Restaurants**
   - Many traditional places now have vegetarian options, including grilled veggies and cheese dishes.

Food Markets

Buenos Aires' markets are great for tasting local food and seeing everyday life.

1. **San Telmo Market**
   - Offers street food, artisanal products, and antiques. **Cost**: Street food costs ARS 800 - 2,000 ($2.50 - $6 USD).
2. **Mercado de Belgrano**
   - A local market with fresh produce and gourmet foods. **Cost**: Products range from ARS 500 - 2,500 ($1.50 - $7 USD).

3. **Mercado de San Nicolás**
   - Has a mix of local food stalls and international cuisine. **Cost**: Meals cost ARS 1,500 - 3,500 ($4.50 - $10 USD).

Wine Tasting

Argentina is famous for its **Malbec** wine, and there are many places in Buenos Aires to sample local wines.

1. **Top Wine Bars**
   - **Pain et Vin** (Palermo): A wine bar that pairs wines with freshly baked bread. **Cost**: Wine tastings range from ARS 5,000 - 8,000 ($15 - $25 USD).
   - **Vino el Cine** (Palermo): Combines wine tasting with classic Argentine movies. **Cost**: ARS 4,000 - 6,500 ($12 - $19 USD).
2. **Wine Tasting Tours**
   - **Anuva Wines**: Hosts wine tastings that focus on small Argentine wineries. **Cost**: ARS 10,000 - 15,000 ($30 - $45 USD).

Local Sweets and Bakeries

Buenos Aires has many bakeries offering delicious treats.

1. **Top Bakeries**
   - **Confitería La Rambla** (Recoleta): Known for its pastries. **Cost**: Pastries cost ARS 300 - 800 ($1 - $2.50 USD).
   - **El Progreso** (Palermo): An old-style bakery famous for its croissants and cakes. **Cost**: ARS 500 - 1,200 ($1.50 - $4 USD).
2. **Must-Try Treats**
   - **Alfajores**: Try these sweet cookies filled with dulce de leche. **Cost**: ARS 500 - 1,000 ($1.50 - $3 USD) each.
   - **Churros with Chocolate**: Enjoy crispy churros dipped in hot chocolate at **Café La Giralda**. **Cost**: ARS 1,500 - 2,500 ($4.50 - $7.50 USD).

Chapter 9: Nightlife and Entertainment

Buenos Aires is a city that truly comes alive after dark, offering a variety of nightlife experiences that cater to all tastes. From sophisticated cocktail bars and underground speakeasies to vibrant nightclubs and live music venues, the city has something for everyone. Buenos Aires' reputation as the "Paris of South America" is evident in its diverse entertainment options, blending European sophistication with a distinctly Latin flair.

Best Bars and Speakeasies

Buenos Aires is home to some of the best cocktail bars in Latin America, with skilled bartenders crafting inventive drinks that push the boundaries of mixology. The city's speakeasies, often hidden behind unmarked doors or disguised as other businesses, offer a unique nightlife experience.

- **Florería Atlántico**

Located in the upscale Recoleta neighborhood, Florería Atlántico is a world-renowned bar, regularly featured on lists of the world's best bars. The entrance is through a flower shop, adding to its speakeasy appeal. Once inside, you'll find a chic basement bar that serves cocktails inspired by the different immigrant communities that have shaped Buenos Aires.

- ○ **Location**: Arroyo 872, Recoleta
- ○ **Pricing**: Cocktails range from $10 to $15
- ○ **Website**: www.floreriaatlantico.com.ar
- **The Harrison Speakeasy**

Situated behind the façade of Nicky NY Sushi in Palermo, The Harrison Speakeasy takes inspiration from the 1920s Prohibition era. The interior is elegant, with leather seating and dim lighting that create a cozy atmosphere. Access is granted through a hidden door in the restaurant, and reservations are essential due to its exclusivity.

- o **Location**: Malabia 1764, Palermo
- o **Pricing**: Entrance fee around $20 (includes a welcome cocktail); cocktails range from $15 to $20
- o **Website**: www.theharrison.com.ar
- **878 Bar (Ocho Siete Ocho)**

One of the city's original speakeasy-style bars, 878 Bar is hidden behind an unassuming façade in Villa Crespo. Known for its relaxed atmosphere and excellent cocktails, the bar also has an extensive selection of whiskeys and craft beers. The unpretentious vibe makes it a popular choice among locals and tourists alike.

- o **Location**: Thames 878, Villa Crespo
- o **Pricing**: Cocktails range from $8 to $12, beer from $5 to $8
- o **Website**: www.878bar.com.ar

- **La Puerta Roja**

Located in the San Telmo district, La Puerta Roja is a lively bar that offers a mix of craft cocktails, beers, and classic Argentine bar food. The bar is known for its friendly, laid-back atmosphere and is a favorite among expats.

- **Location**: Chacabuco 733, San Telmo
- **Pricing**: Cocktails start at $6, beers from $4
- **No official website**

The City's Vibrant Nightclub Scene

Buenos Aires is famous for its late-night party culture, with nightclubs that don't get busy until well after midnight. The music ranges from electronic and techno to cumbia and reggaeton, catering to diverse tastes. Here are some of the best spots to experience the city's nightclub scene:

- **Crobar**
  A staple of Buenos Aires' electronic music scene, Crobar is located in the Palermo district and regularly hosts international DJs. The club features a spacious dance floor and impressive sound system, making it a favorite destination for fans of techno and house music.
  - **Location**: Av. del Libertador 3886, Palermo
  - **Pricing**: Entrance fees range from $10 to $30, depending on the event; drinks from $6

- o **Website**: www.crobar.com.ar
- **Kika Club**

  Located in the heart of Palermo, Kika Club is popular for its diverse music nights, ranging from electronic and hip hop to reggaeton. The club attracts a young crowd, and its weekly theme nights keep the atmosphere fresh and exciting.
  - o **Location**: Honduras 5339, Palermo
  - o **Pricing**: Entrance fees range from $5 to $15, with drinks priced from $6
  - o **Website**: www.kikaclub.com.ar
- **Bahrein**

  One of the most iconic nightclubs in Buenos Aires, Bahrein is housed in a historic building in the city center. The club has multiple dance floors with different music genres on each level, including electronic, hip hop, and funk. It is particularly known for its underground techno scene.
  - o **Location**: Lavalle 345, Microcentro
  - o **Pricing**: Entrance fees range from $10 to $25, drinks from $5
  - o **Website**: www.bahreinba.com
- **Rose in Rio**

  Situated along the Costanera Norte, Rose in Rio offers a mix of music genres with a large outdoor area overlooking the Río de la Plata. It's perfect for those who want to enjoy the night air while dancing to reggaeton, cumbia, and Latin pop.
  - o **Location**: Av. Rafael Obligado 1221, Costanera Norte
  - o **Pricing**: Entrance fees typically range from $10 to $20, with cocktails from $8
  - o **Website**: www.roseinrio.com.ar

Live Music Venues: From Jazz to Folklore

Buenos Aires has a rich musical heritage that extends beyond tango, with a thriving live music scene that spans jazz, rock, and traditional Argentine folklore. Here are some top venues to catch live music:

- **Thelonious Club**

  Known as one of the city's best jazz bars, Thelonious Club in Palermo is an intimate venue that hosts local and international jazz musicians. The laid-back atmosphere and high-quality performances make it a great spot for jazz enthusiasts.
  - o **Location**: Nicaragua 5549, Palermo
  - o **Pricing**: Cover charge around $8-$12; drinks from $6
  - o **Website**: www.thelonious.com.ar
- **La Trastienda**

  Located in the historic San Telmo neighborhood, La Trastienda is a versatile live music venue that features performances from rock bands, folk musicians, and even international acts. The venue's flexible seating arrangements allow for different types of events, from seated concerts to standing-room shows.

- Location: Balcarce 460, San Telmo
- Pricing: Tickets range from $15 to $50, depending on the artist
- Website: www.latrastienda.com

- **Centro Cultural Torquato Tasso**
For a taste of traditional Argentine folk music, head to Centro Cultural Torquato Tasso. The venue often hosts live performances of folklore and tango, offering a more traditional cultural experience.
  - Location: Defensa 1575, San Telmo
  - Pricing: Entrance fees range from $10 to $25, drinks from $5
  - Website: www.torquatotasso.com.ar
- **Cafe Vinilo**
A beloved spot for lovers of acoustic music and small concerts, Café Vinilo focuses on Argentine and Latin American folk music. The intimate setting and high-quality sound make it an ideal place to experience authentic musical performances.
  - Location: Gorriti 3780, Palermo
  - Pricing: Cover charge around $10-$15; drinks from $5
  - Website: www.cafevinilo.com.ar

Theater Scene: Must-See Performances

Buenos Aires is a hub for performing arts in South America, with a theater scene that rivals those of New York and London. Whether you're interested in classic plays, avant-garde productions, or tango shows, the city's theaters offer a variety of performances.

- **Teatro Colón**
Regarded as one of the world's most beautiful opera houses, Teatro Colón is a must-visit for anyone interested in the performing arts. The venue regularly hosts opera, ballet, and classical music concerts, with performances by renowned international and local artists.
  - Location: Cerrito 628, Microcentro
  - Pricing: Tickets range from $20 to $150, depending on the show
  - Website: www.teatrocolon.org.ar
- **Teatro San Martín**
Teatro San Martín is one of Buenos Aires' most important cultural institutions, offering a wide range of performances, including drama, dance, and film screenings. The building itself is a work of art, with a modernist design and multiple performance spaces.
  - Location: Av. Corrientes 1530, Microcentro

- **Pricing**: Tickets range from $10 to $40, depending on the production
- **Website**: www.complejoteatral.gob.ar
- **Paseo La Plaza**

  A multi-theater complex located on the bustling Avenida Corrientes, Paseo La Plaza is home to a variety of shows, from stand-up comedy to contemporary theater productions. Its central location makes it an ideal spot to catch a show and then head out for a late dinner.
  - **Location**: Av. Corrientes 1660, Microcentro
  - **Pricing**: Tickets range from $15 to $50
  - **Website**: www.paseolaplaza.com.ar
- **El Galpón de Guevara**

  Known for its avant-garde productions and contemporary performances, El Galpón de Guevara is a more experimental theater that attracts fans of modern and alternative performing arts.
  - **Location**: Guevara 326, Chacarita
  - **Pricing**: Tickets usually range from $10 to $30
  - **Website**: www.elgalpondeguevara.com.ar

Chapter 10: Shopping in Buenos Aires

Buenos Aires is a great place for shopping, with a mix of luxury boutiques, traditional markets, and unique stores. Whether you're looking for high-end fashion, local souvenirs, or antiques, there's something for everyone. This chapter will guide you through the top shopping spots, including where to find souvenirs, fashion boutiques, antiques, and shopping centers.

Unique Souvenirs and Where to Find Them

Buenos Aires has plenty of unique souvenirs beyond the usual keychains and magnets. Here are some special items and where to buy them:

- **Leather Goods**
  - Argentina is famous for its quality leather products like jackets, belts, wallets, and bags.
  - **Where to Buy**:
    - **Casa López** (stores in Palermo and Recoleta) is known for its fine leather items.
    - **Murillo 666**: This street in Villa Crespo has many shops selling good leather items at reasonable prices.
- **Mate Cups and Bombillas**
  - Drinking mate (a type of herbal tea) is a big part of Argentine culture. You can buy a mate cup and straw to take home.
  - **Where to Buy**:

- **Maté & Co** in Palermo sells well-made mate cups made from different materials like wood and ceramic.
    - **Price**: $10-$40 USD depending on the style.
- **Alfajores and Dulce de Leche**
    - Alfajores (cookies filled with caramel-like dulce de leche) are classic Argentine treats. They make great gifts.
    - **Where to Buy**:
        - **Havanna** (stores all over the city) is the most famous alfajor brand in Argentina.
            - **Price**: About $6-$12 USD per box.
        - **El Viejo Oso Dulce** in San Telmo sells more artisanal options.
- **Handmade Silver Jewelry**
    - Argentina is known for its silver craftsmanship, and you can find beautiful handmade jewelry.
    - **Where to Buy**:
        - **Plata Nativa** in Recoleta specializes in silver jewelry with unique designs.
- **Gaucho Knives (Facón)**
    - Gaucho knives are traditional and often handmade with decorative designs.
    - **Where to Buy**:
        - **La Casa del Facón** in San Telmo has authentic handmade knives.

Boutique Shopping in Palermo and Recoleta

Palermo and Recoleta are great neighborhoods for shopping, known for stylish boutiques and designer stores.

- **Palermo Soho**
    - This bohemian neighborhood is filled with boutiques from local designers. You'll find shops selling everything from vintage clothes to the latest fashion trends.
    - **Boutiques to Visit**:
        - **Rapsodia**: A store with boho-style clothing.
            - **Price Range**: Clothes cost around $50-$150 USD.
            - **Website**: https://www.rapsodia.com.ar
        - **Cora Groppo**: Known for creative and unique clothing designs.
            - **Price Range**: $80-$300 USD.
            - **Website**: https://www.coragroppo.com
        - **Peuque**: Specializes in denim and casual wear.
            - **Website**: https://www.peuque.com.ar

- **Recoleta**
  - This neighborhood is known for luxury shopping and upscale boutiques.
  - **Boutiques to Visit**:
    - **Patricia Profumo**: A high-end fashion designer specializing in dresses.
      - **Price Range**: Dresses cost from $200-$1000 USD.
    - **Silvia & Mario Leather**: A family-owned store that customizes leather jackets and bags.
      - **Website**: https://www.silviaymario.com

The Best Local Designers and Fashion Brands

Buenos Aires is full of talented designers who create unique clothes inspired by local culture. Here are some brands to check out:

- **Benito Fernández**
  - This designer is famous for his colorful and bold clothes.
  - **Where to Find**: The showroom is in Recoleta.
  - **Price Range**: Dresses start at $300 USD.
- **Jessica Trosman**
  - A well-known designer who uses unusual materials for creative clothing.
  - **Where to Find**: Trosman stores in Palermo.
  - **Price Range**: $150-$500 USD.
- **Ginebra**
  - A modern brand mixing classic tailoring with contemporary style.
  - **Where to Find**: Ginebra stores in Palermo Soho and other locations.
  - **Website**: https://www.ginebrabsas.com.ar
- **Martin Churba - Tramando**
  - Tramando blends art and fashion in its designs, offering stylish and unique clothes.
  - **Where to Find**: Tramando stores in Palermo.
  - **Price Range**: $100-$400 USD.
  - **Website**: https://www.tramando.com.ar

Antique Hunting in San Telmo

San Telmo is one of Buenos Aires' oldest neighborhoods and is well-known for antiques and vintage shops.

- **San Telmo Market (Mercado de San Telmo)**

- This market has been around since 1897 and offers antiques, collectibles, and vintage items.
- **Location**: Defensa 961, San Telmo.
- **Open Hours**: Open daily, with more stalls on Sundays during the San Telmo Feria.
- **Things to Find**: Vintage clothes, antique furniture, and old photos.
- **San Telmo Feria (Sunday Market)**
  - Every Sunday, Defensa Street turns into a market with antiques, crafts, and street performers.
  - **Location**: Defensa Street, from Plaza Dorrego to Avenida San Juan.
  - **Things to Find**: Handmade crafts, antiques, and tango performances.
  - **Website**: San Telmo Feria
- **Antique Shops on Defensa Street**
  - You'll find many antique shops open all week along Defensa Street.
  - **Shops to Visit**:
    - **Galería El Solar de French**: An antique gallery with several dealers.
    - **Antigüedades Mariano**: Focuses on Argentine collectibles from the 19th and 20th centuries.

Shopping Malls and Outlet Centers

For those who prefer modern shopping centers, Buenos Aires has many malls and outlets with both local and international brands.

- **Galerías Pacífico**
  - This iconic mall is located in a historic building with beautiful murals on the ceiling. It offers a mix of local and international brands.
  - **Location**: Av. Córdoba 550, Microcentro.
  - **Website**: https://www.galeriaspacifico.com.ar
  - **Things to Find**: Luxury brands like **La Martina** and international names like **Nike**.
- **Alto Palermo Shopping**
  - Located in Palermo, this mall has a variety of stores from affordable brands to high-end shops.
  - **Location**: Av. Santa Fe 3253, Palermo.
  - **Website**: https://www.altopalermo.com.ar
  - **Things to Find**: Stores like **Zara**, **Adidas**, and **Ricky Sarkany**.
- **Distrito Arcos Outlet**
  - An outdoor outlet mall offering discounts on well-known brands. It's great for finding bargains while enjoying the open-air setting.

- **Location**: Paraguay 4979, Palermo.
- **Website**: Distrito Arcos
- **Pricing**: Expect 30-60% off regular prices.

- **Dot Baires Shopping**
  - This modern shopping center in Núñez has stores, dining, and entertainment options.
  - **Location**: Vedia 3626, Núñez.
  - **Website**: Dot Baires
  - **Things to Find**: Brands like **Tommy Hilfiger**, **MAC Cosmetics**, and local favorites like **Rapsodia**.

Chapter 11: Day Trips and Excursions

Buenos Aires offers plenty to explore within its borders, but some of the best experiences lie just beyond the city limits. Here's a guide to the top day trips and excursions, covering nearby towns, cultural experiences, and scenic retreats. Whether you're interested in a historical outing, rural landscapes, or a day at the beach, these destinations are perfect for expanding your Argentine adventure.

Tigre Delta: River Cruises and Market Visits

Location: Tigre is located about 30 km (19 miles) north of Buenos Aires, easily accessible by train, bus, or car.

The Tigre Delta is a network of islands and waterways formed by the Paraná River, offering a unique escape from the bustling city. It's renowned for its lush scenery, charming houses on stilts, and a range of outdoor activities.

- **Activities**: The most popular way to explore Tigre is by taking a river cruise. Various options are available, from public water taxis (**lancha colectiva**) to private boat tours and catamaran cruises. These tours provide stunning views of the delta's natural beauty and insight into the local lifestyle.
  - **River Cruise Pricing**: Public boat rides start at **ARS 1,500** (around USD 4) for short trips. Private boat tours cost from **ARS 8,000** (USD 22) per hour.
  - **Boat Tour Websites**: https://www.deltaboats.com.ar, https://www.sturlaviajes.com

- **Puerto de Frutos Market**: Another highlight of Tigre is the Puerto de Frutos, a bustling riverside market selling everything from handcrafted goods to fresh produce. The market's atmosphere, with its lively stalls and colorful displays, makes it a great spot to shop for souvenirs or enjoy local snacks.
- **Parque de la Costa**: Families can visit this amusement park, offering a variety of rides and attractions, from roller coasters to water slides.
  - **Park Entrance Fee**: From **ARS 3,000** (USD 8) for basic entry.
  - **Website**: https://www.parquedelacosta.com.ar

Getting There: The most convenient way is by taking the **Mitre Line train** from Retiro Station to Tigre, which takes about **50 minutes**. Tickets cost around **ARS 50** (USD 0.15).

Colonia del Sacramento, Uruguay: A Historical Getaway

Location: Colonia del Sacramento is located across the Río de la Plata, approximately 50 km (31 miles) from Buenos Aires.

A UNESCO World Heritage Site, Colonia del Sacramento is one of Uruguay's oldest towns, famous for its cobblestone streets, colonial architecture, and historic sites. This picturesque town offers a charming day trip filled with history, beautiful waterfront views, and a slower pace of life.

- **Activities**:
  - **Walking Tour of the Historic Quarter**: The old town's cobblestone streets, lined with colorful houses, evoke a bygone era. Key attractions include the **Basilica del Santísimo Sacramento**, the **Lighthouse and Plaza Mayor**, and the historic **Portón de Campo**.
  - **Museo Portugués**: Learn about Colonia's Portuguese origins through artifacts and exhibits.
    - **Entrance Fee**: Approximately **UYU 150** (USD 4).
- **Dining and Cafés**: Colonia offers numerous quaint eateries where you can enjoy local cuisine, such as **chivito** (Uruguayan steak sandwich) and **medialunas** (sweet croissants).

Getting There: The most popular way to reach Colonia is by ferry from Buenos Aires. Several ferry companies operate daily services, including **Buquebus** and **Colonia Express**.

- **Ferry Pricing**: Round-trip tickets range from **ARS 30,000** to **ARS 60,000** (USD 80-160), depending on the season and service.
- **Website**: https://www.buquebus.com, https://www.coloniaexpress.com

Gaucho Ranch Experiences: Estancias Near Buenos Aires

Location: The estancias (ranches) are typically located in the Pampas region, within a 1-2 hour drive from Buenos Aires.

Experiencing an **estancia** is an opportunity to embrace Argentina's rural lifestyle and gaucho (cowboy) culture. These ranches offer a combination of horseback riding, traditional **asado** (barbecue), folk music, and dance performances.

- **Activities**:
  - **Horseback Riding and Carriage Rides**: Enjoy a ride through the Pampas with experienced guides.
  - **Gaucho Show**: Many estancias offer cultural performances showcasing traditional gaucho skills, including horse riding tricks and **malambo** (a folk dance).
  - **Traditional Asado Lunch**: Guests are treated to an authentic Argentine barbecue featuring meats, grilled vegetables, and local wines.
- **Popular Estancias Near Buenos Aires**:
  - **Estancia La Cinacina** (San Antonio de Areco): Known for its beautiful grounds and traditional atmosphere. Prices start at **ARS 15,000** (USD 40) for a day visit, including activities and lunch.
    - **Website**: https://www.lacinacina.com.ar
  - **Estancia El Ombú de Areco**: A historic ranch offering overnight stays and day visits. Day trips cost around **ARS 25,000** (USD 70) per person.
    - **Website**: https://www.estanciaelombu.com

Getting There: Travel to the estancias can be arranged through tour companies offering private transfers or by renting a car for a self-drive experience. Buses from **Retiro Bus Terminal** to nearby towns such as **San Antonio de Areco** are also an option.

The Beaches of Mar del Plata and Pinamar

Location: Mar del Plata is located about 400 km (250 miles) south of Buenos Aires, while Pinamar is approximately 340 km (210 miles) from the city.

For beach lovers, a trip to **Mar del Plata** or **Pinamar** is an ideal getaway. These coastal towns offer sandy beaches, lively nightlife, and various outdoor activities.

- **Mar del Plata**: The most popular beach resort town in Argentina, known for its wide sandy beaches, seafood restaurants, and vibrant atmosphere.

- ○ **Activities**: Beach relaxation, surfing, and visiting the **Aquarium Mar del Plata**.
    - ■ **Aquarium Entrance Fee**: From **ARS 5,000** (USD 13).
    - ■ **Website**: https://www.aquarium.com.ar
  - ○ **Nightlife**: Mar del Plata is famous for its bars, nightclubs, and casinos, such as **Casino Central**, a landmark of the city.
- **Pinamar**: Known for its upscale atmosphere and pine-lined streets, Pinamar is a great spot for those looking for a more relaxed and exclusive beach experience.
  - ○ **Activities**: Enjoying water sports like kite surfing, windsurfing, or renting **ATVs** for beach rides.
  - ○ **Beach Equipment Rentals**: Beach chair and umbrella rentals typically cost around **ARS 4,000** (USD 10) per day.

Getting There:

- **By Bus**: Regular buses run from **Retiro Bus Terminal** to Mar del Plata and Pinamar. The journey takes **5-6 hours**, with ticket prices ranging from **ARS 10,000** to **ARS 15,000** (USD 27-40).
- **By Car**: Renting a car allows for more flexibility, especially if planning to visit multiple beach towns.

Exploring the Pampas: Rural Landscapes and History

Location: The Pampas region lies west and southwest of Buenos Aires and encompasses vast grasslands ideal for farming and ranching.

The Pampas are not just about the gauchos but also offer a glimpse into Argentina's agricultural heritage and traditional rural life. Visitors can experience the open countryside, explore quaint towns, and learn about the farming lifestyle.

- **Highlights**:
  - ○ **San Antonio de Areco**: This charming town, known as the cradle of gaucho traditions, is perfect for a day trip. Visit the **Museo Gauchesco Ricardo Güiraldes** and stroll through the picturesque streets.
    - ■ **Museum Entrance Fee**: Approximately **ARS 1,000** (USD 2.70).
  - ○ **Luján**: Famous for its **Basilica of Our Lady of Luján**, a beautiful neo-Gothic church and a major pilgrimage site.
    - ■ **Basilica Entrance**: Free.
    - ■ **Website**: https://www.basilicadelujan.org.ar

Getting There:

- **By Bus or Train**: The towns in the Pampas are accessible via bus from Buenos Aires. **San Antonio de Areco** is about a **2-hour drive** from Buenos Aires, while **Luján** is about **1 hour** away.

La Plata: Architecture, Museums, and Cathedral Visits

Location: La Plata is situated about 60 km (37 miles) southeast of Buenos Aires.

La Plata, the capital of Buenos Aires Province, is a planned city known for its unique architecture, wide streets, and cultural attractions. Founded in 1882, the city is rich in history and offers plenty of sites for visitors.

- **Key Attractions**:
  - **La Plata Cathedral**: One of the largest and most beautiful neo-Gothic cathedrals in South America, featuring stunning stained glass windows and a panoramic tower view.
    - **Entrance Fee for Tower Access: ARS 300** (USD 0.80).
    - **Website**: https://www.catedraldelaplata.com.ar
  - **Museo de La Plata**: A fascinating museum dedicated to natural history and anthropology, featuring dinosaur skeletons and cultural artifacts.
    - **Entrance Fee: ARS 2,000** (USD 5.50).
    - **Website**: Museo de La Plata
  - **Republica de los Niños**: A children's theme park that resembles a miniature city, complete with government buildings, a bank, and a courthouse. It's considered one of the inspirations for Disneyland.
    - **Entrance Fee: ARS 1,500** (USD 4).

Getting There:

- **By Train**: The **Roca Line** runs from **Constitución Station** in Buenos Aires to La Plata, taking about **1.5 hours**.
- **By Bus**: Frequent buses connect Buenos Aires with La Plata, with ticket prices starting at **ARS 500** (USD 1.40).

Chapter 12: Buenos Aires on a Budget

Buenos Aires is an exciting and vibrant city known for its rich culture, passionate tango, and delicious cuisine. While it offers luxury experiences, the city also provides plenty of ways for budget travelers to enjoy its charms without breaking the bank. This chapter covers affordable accommodations, free and low-cost activities, cheap eats, transportation tips, and budget-friendly tango lessons and shows, helping you experience Buenos Aires on a budget.

Affordable Accommodations: Hostels and Budget Hotels

Finding budget-friendly accommodations in Buenos Aires is easy, as the city offers a range of hostels and budget hotels that cater to all types of travelers. Here are some recommended places:

1. **Milhouse Hostel Hipo**
   - **Location**: Hipólito Yrigoyen 959, San Telmo
   - **Highlights**: A popular hostel known for its social atmosphere, Milhouse Hipo is great for young travelers and backpackers. It offers private rooms and dormitories, a bar, a rooftop terrace, and daily activities, such as city tours and tango lessons.
   - **Pricing**: Dorm beds start at $15 per night, while private rooms are available from $40.
   - **Website**: https://www.milhousehostel.com
2. **America del Sur Hostel Buenos Aires**
   - **Location**: Chacabuco 718, San Telmo
   - **Highlights**: A modern hostel with a relaxed vibe, located in the historic San Telmo neighborhood. It offers free Wi-Fi, shared kitchens, and a BBQ area. Guests can also enjoy social events and city tours organized by the hostel.
   - **Pricing**: Dorm beds start at $18 per night, while private rooms range from $50 to $70.
   - **Website**: americahostel.com
3. **Circus Hostel & Hotel**
   - **Location**: Chacabuco 1020, San Telmo
   - **Highlights**: Circus Hostel & Hotel is a mix of budget hotel and hostel accommodations. It features a swimming pool, free breakfast, and a lively atmosphere with social events. It's a good choice for travelers who want a bit more comfort while still keeping costs down.
   - **Pricing**: Dorm beds start at $17 per night, with private rooms from $45.

- Website: circushostel.com.ar
4. **Hotel Ibis Buenos Aires Obelisco**
    - **Location**: Avenida Corrientes 1344, Microcentro
    - **Highlights**: This budget hotel is part of the well-known Ibis chain, offering reliable, clean, and affordable accommodations. It's located near the Obelisco, making it an ideal base for exploring the city.
    - **Pricing**: Rooms start at $50 per night.
    - **Website**: ibis.accor.com
5. **Che Juan Hostel BA**
    - **Location**: Maipú 306, Microcentro
    - **Highlights**: Located in the heart of the city, Che Juan Hostel is known for its excellent location and cozy atmosphere. It has comfortable dorms and private rooms, a communal kitchen, and common areas for socializing.
    - **Pricing**: Dorm beds start at $16 per night, while private rooms start at $38.
    - **Website**: chejuanhostel.com

These accommodations provide a balance between affordability, comfort, and social experiences, making them ideal choices for budget-conscious travelers.

Free and Low-Cost Activities in the City

Buenos Aires offers a variety of attractions and experiences that are either free or inexpensive. Here are some must-visit spots for travelers on a budget:

1. **Explore Plaza de Mayo and Casa Rosada**
    - **Location**: Bolívar, Microcentro
    - **Highlights**: This historic square is surrounded by iconic buildings like the Casa Rosada (Presidential Palace), the Metropolitan Cathedral, and the Cabildo. It's a great place to learn about Argentina's history and see where many political events have taken place.
    - **Pricing**: Free. Guided tours of Casa Rosada are also free but require online reservations.
    - **Website**: casarosada.gob.ar
2. **Visit Recoleta Cemetery**
    - **Location**: Junín 1760, Recoleta
    - **Highlights**: Recoleta Cemetery is one of the city's most famous attractions, known for its elaborate mausoleums and tombs, including that of Eva Perón. It's a fascinating place to explore and learn about Argentina's history.
    - **Pricing**: Free.
3. **Wander Through San Telmo Market**

- Location: Defensa 961, San Telmo
- **Highlights**: The San Telmo Market is an indoor market with a mix of food stalls, antiques, and local crafts. It's a great spot to experience the local culture, try some traditional street food, and shop for unique souvenirs.
- **Pricing**: Free to enter. Prices for food and goods vary.

4. **Discover Street Art in Palermo**
   - **Location**: Palermo Soho and Palermo Hollywood
   - **Highlights**: Buenos Aires is famous for its vibrant street art scene, and Palermo is one of the best neighborhoods to explore this urban canvas. Take a self-guided walk to discover colorful murals and graffiti that tell stories about the city's culture and history.
   - **Pricing**: Free. Guided street art tours are available for $15-$20.

5. **Attend a Free Tango Show at La Glorieta**
   - **Location**: Barrancas de Belgrano Park, Belgrano
   - **Highlights**: La Glorieta is an open-air venue where locals dance the tango on weekends. It's a great opportunity to watch dancers perform and even join in if you're feeling adventurous.
   - **Pricing**: Free. Donations are appreciated.

6. **Relax at Parque Tres de Febrero**
   - **Location**: Avenida Libertador y Sarmiento, Palermo
   - **Highlights**: This beautiful park features lakes, rose gardens, and sculptures, offering a peaceful retreat from the bustling city. It's perfect for a picnic, a leisurely walk, or renting a paddleboat on the lake.
   - **Pricing**: Free to enter. Paddleboat rentals start at $5 per hour.

7. **Visit the Buenos Aires Ecological Reserve**
   - **Location**: Avenida Tristán Achával Rodríguez 1550, Puerto Madero
   - **Highlights**: Located near the city's waterfront, this natural reserve provides a contrast to the urban landscape. It's a great place for birdwatching, cycling, or hiking along the trails.
   - **Pricing**: Free.

These activities provide a mix of cultural experiences and outdoor adventures, allowing you to enjoy the city's rich atmosphere without spending much.

Cheap Eats: Where to Find Great Food for Less

Buenos Aires is a paradise for food lovers, with a wide range of budget-friendly options for sampling local flavors. Here are some places to enjoy delicious food without breaking the bank:

1. **El Banco Rojo**
   - **Location**: Bolivar 866, San Telmo
   - **Highlights**: A popular spot among locals, El Banco Rojo serves hearty portions of street food-inspired dishes such as empanadas, sandwiches, and tacos. Their signature dish, the "Choripan," is a must-try.
   - **Pricing**: Meals start at $5.
2. **Pizzeria Güerrin**
   - **Location**: Avenida Corrientes 1368, Microcentro
   - **Highlights**: Founded in 1932, Güerrin is a legendary pizzeria on Corrientes Avenue. Known for its thick-crust "fugazza" pizza, this place is perfect for grabbing a slice on the go or dining in.
   - **Pricing**: Pizza slices start at $2. Whole pizzas range from $8 to $15.
   - **Website**: https://www.pizzeriaguerrin.com.ar
3. **Nuestra Parrilla**
   - **Location**: Carlos Calvo 471, San Telmo
   - **Highlights**: A small, family-run parrilla (grill) in San Telmo that serves authentic Argentine street food. Their choripán and steak sandwiches are popular among budget travelers.
   - **Pricing**: Meals start at $4.
4. **Las Cabras**
   - **Location**: Fitz Roy 1795, Palermo
   - **Highlights**: A well-known parrilla in Palermo offering affordable Argentine cuisine. Their "Gran Bife" (large steak) is a popular choice and big enough to share.
   - **Pricing**: Main dishes range from $8 to $15.
5. **La Cocina**
   - **Location**: Pueyrredón 1508, Recoleta
   - **Highlights**: Famous for its homemade empanadas, La Cocina is a small restaurant offering traditional fillings such as beef, chicken, and cheese.
   - **Pricing**: Empanadas start at $1.50 each.

These eateries allow you to enjoy authentic Argentine cuisine without spending a fortune, making Buenos Aires a great destination for food lovers on a budget.

Tips for Saving on Transportation and Entrance Fees

Buenos Aires offers several ways to keep transportation and entry fees low while still exploring the city:

1. **Use the SUBE Card for Public Transport**

- The SUBE card is a rechargeable card that can be used on buses, the Subte (metro), and trains across the city. It's the cheapest way to get around, with fares starting at $0.20 per trip.
  - **Where to Get It**: Available at Subte stations, kiosks, and convenience stores.
2. **Walk or Bike Around the City**
   - Many of Buenos Aires' attractions are within walking distance of each other, especially in neighborhoods like Palermo, San Telmo, and Recoleta. The city also has a bike-sharing program called **Ecobici**, which is free for tourists for up to one hour per ride.
   - **Website**: ecobici.buenosaires.gob.ar
3. **Free Museum Days**
   - Many museums, such as the **Museo Nacional de Bellas Artes**, offer free admission on certain days, often on Wednesdays or the first Sunday of the month. Plan your museum visits accordingly to save on entrance fees.
   - **Website**: mnba.gob.ar
4. **Discounted Tango Shows**
   - Some tango venues offer discounts for early bookings or last-minute deals. Check local listings, such as **Tango Map Guide** or **Hoy Milonga**, for discounted or free tango events.
   - **Website**: https://www.hoy-milonga.com

Budget-Friendly Tango Lessons and Shows

Experiencing tango is a must in Buenos Aires, but it doesn't have to be expensive. Here are some budget-friendly options:

1. **La Catedral Club**
   - **Location**: Sarmiento 4006, Almagro
   - **Highlights**: Known for its relaxed vibe and vintage decor, La Catedral offers tango lessons and milongas for beginners and experienced dancers alike.
   - **Pricing**: Tango lessons start at $6, and milonga entrance fees range from $4 to $10.
   - **Website**: https://www.lacatedralclub.com
2. **Confitería Ideal**
   - **Location**: Suipacha 384, Microcentro
   - **Highlights**: An iconic tango venue that hosts affordable classes and milongas in a historic setting. It's a great place to learn the basics of tango while soaking up the atmosphere.
   - **Pricing**: Classes start at $8.
3. **La Glorieta Milonga**

- **Location**: Barrancas de Belgrano Park, Belgrano
- **Highlights**: An open-air milonga held in a charming gazebo, where you can watch tango for free and even join in. Classes are available for those interested in learning the dance.
- **Pricing**: Free, with donations appreciated.

Chapter 13: Luxury Travel in Buenos Aires

Buenos Aires, a city where European elegance meets Latin American charm, offers a plethora of luxurious experiences that cater to travelers seeking the finer things in life. This chapter dives into high-end accommodations, exclusive tours, luxury shopping, gourmet dining, and indulgent spa retreats, providing a guide to experiencing Buenos Aires in the most opulent way possible.

Top 5-Star Hotels and High-End Resorts

Buenos Aires boasts a range of upscale accommodations, from historic palaces to contemporary luxury hotels, ensuring a comfortable and lavish stay.

1. **Alvear Palace Hotel**

- ○ **Location**: Recoleta, Avenida Alvear 1891

- ○ **Description**: One of Buenos Aires' most iconic luxury hotels, the Alvear Palace Hotel exudes European elegance with French-inspired architecture and opulent interiors. Established in 1932, it features 192 rooms and suites, each decorated with Louis XVI-style furnishings. Guests can enjoy a butler service, afternoon tea in the elegant L'Orangerie, and fine dining at the award-winning French restaurant, La Bourgogne.
- ○ **Pricing**: Rooms start at approximately $450 per night, with suites exceeding $1,000 per night.
- ○ **Website**: www.alvearpalace.com

2. **Four Seasons Hotel Buenos Aires**

- **Location**: Retiro, Posadas 1086/88

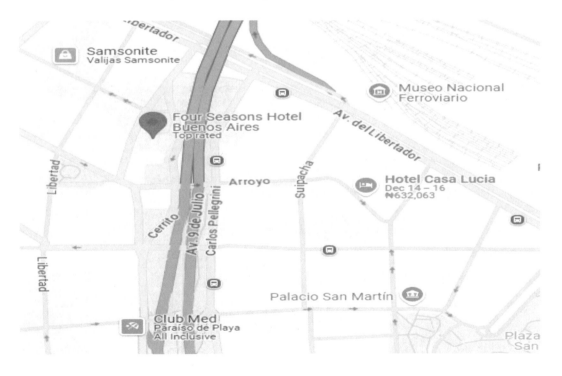

- **Description**: Located in the upscale Retiro district, the Four Seasons Hotel seamlessly blends modern luxury with historic charm, featuring a Belle

Époque-style mansion and a contemporary high-rise tower. The hotel offers spacious rooms, a pool, and exclusive experiences such as polo lessons. The onsite restaurant, Elena, is one of the best in the city, serving gourmet Argentine cuisine.

- **Pricing**: Rooms start around $600 per night, with premium suites costing over $1,500 per night.
- **Website**: www.fourseasons.com/buenosaires

3. **Palacio Duhau – Park Hyatt Buenos Aires**

- **Location**: Recoleta, Avenida Alvear 1661

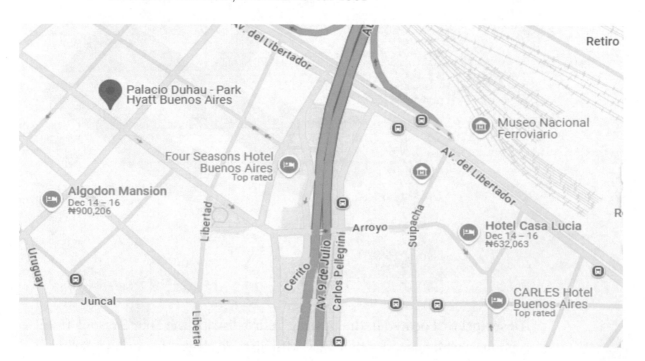

- **Description**: A magnificent blend of old-world charm and modern sophistication, this hotel occupies a beautifully restored 1930s palace and a modern wing. Guests can stroll through the landscaped gardens, relax in the Ahín Wellness & Spa, or dine at Duhau Restaurante & Vinoteca, which offers an extensive wine selection and gourmet Argentine dishes.
- **Pricing**: Rates start at $550 per night, with luxury suites priced at over $1,200 per night.
- **Website**: www.hyatt.com

4. **Faena Hotel Buenos Aires**

- **Location**: Puerto Madero, Martha Salotti 445

- **Description**: A unique and artistic luxury hotel designed by Philippe Starck, the Faena offers an eclectic experience in the trendy Puerto Madero district. The hotel's red-themed El Bistro restaurant and the celebrated Rojo Tango show make it a cultural hotspot. The Faena Spa offers wellness treatments inspired by ancient healing rituals.
- **Pricing**: Rooms start at $450 per night, with suites available from $900 and up.
- **Website**: www.faena.com

5. **Hotel Madero Buenos Aires**

- **Location**: Puerto Madero, Rosario Vera Peñaloza 360

- **Description**: Combining contemporary design with luxury amenities, Hotel Madero features spacious rooms with balconies, a rooftop spa, and a chic restaurant serving modern Argentine cuisine. Located in the revitalized Puerto Madero area, it provides easy access to waterfront dining and nightlife.
- **Pricing**: Standard rooms start around $250 per night, with suites from $400 per night.
- **Website**: www.hotelmadero.com

Private Tours and Exclusive Experiences

For those who seek to explore Buenos Aires in style, private tours and exclusive experiences offer a unique way to immerse yourself in the city's culture, history, and lifestyle.

1. **Private Polo Lessons and Matches**
   - **Description**: Argentina is famous for its polo culture, and Buenos Aires offers the opportunity to experience it first-hand. Guests can book private lessons with professional players at clubs like **La Estancia El Venado** or **Argentina Polo Day**, located just outside the city. Lessons include an introduction to the sport, practice time, and a chance to play an informal match.
   - **Pricing**: Polo experiences range from $300 to $600 per person, depending on the package.
   - **Website**: www.argentinapoloday.com.ar
2. **Private Tango Show and Dance Lessons**
   - **Description**: Buenos Aires is the birthplace of tango, and a private tango show or dance lesson is a must-do for luxury travelers. Renowned venues like **Rojo Tango** at the Faena Hotel or **Gala Tango** offer intimate performances accompanied by fine dining. Guests can also opt for private dance lessons at tango schools, such as **Escuela Mundial de Tango**.
   - **Pricing**: Tango shows start at $200 per person, with private lessons from $150 per hour.
   - **Website**: www.rojotango.com
3. **Private City Tour with a Personal Guide**
   - **Description**: Customize your city tour with a knowledgeable local guide who can tailor the itinerary to your interests. Visit iconic sites such as the **Teatro Colón**, **Recoleta Cemetery**, **San Telmo**, and **La Boca** while learning about the city's history, architecture, and culture.
   - **Pricing**: Private tours start at $250 for a half-day and $400 for a full-day experience.

- Website: www.buenosaires-tours.com
4. **Exclusive Wine Tasting Experiences**
   - **Description**: Argentina is renowned for its wine, particularly Malbec. Private wine tastings at venues like **Anuva Wines** or visits to local wine bars such as **Vico Wine Bar** can be arranged for a more personalized experience, featuring rare labels and expert sommeliers.
   - **Pricing**: Private tastings range from $100 to $300 per person, depending on the selection.
   - **Website**: www.anuvawines.com

Luxury Shopping: Designer Boutiques and Fine Jewelry

Buenos Aires is a shopping paradise, offering everything from designer boutiques to local artisanal goods.

1. **Patio Bullrich**
   - **Location**: Recoleta, Posadas 1245
   - **Description**: This upscale shopping center features luxury brands like Louis Vuitton, Carolina Herrera, and Rolex, alongside high-end Argentine designers. The elegant architecture and refined atmosphere make it a top destination for luxury shopping.
   - **Website**: www.patiobullrich.com.ar
2. **Galerías Pacífico**
   - **Location**: Microcentro, Florida and Av. Córdoba
   - **Description**: Known for its beautiful murals and architectural splendor, Galerías Pacífico is home to both international luxury brands and local designers. It's an excellent spot for picking up fine jewelry, leather goods, and high-end fashion.
   - **Website**: www.galeriaspacifico.com.ar
3. **Arandu**
   - **Location**: Recoleta, Avenida Alvear 1928
   - **Description**: Specializing in traditional Argentine leather goods, Arandu offers luxury products like handmade belts, boots, saddles, and ponchos. It's a perfect stop for those seeking high-quality, authentic Argentine fashion.
   - **Website**: www.arandu.com.ar
4. **Rabat**
   - **Location**: Recoleta, Av. Alvear 1883
   - **Description**: A prestigious jewelry store known for its fine collections of gold, diamonds, and precious stones. Rabat's bespoke services allow customers to create custom-made pieces.

High-End Dining and Gourmet Experiences

Buenos Aires' food scene is renowned for its beef, but the city also offers gourmet experiences beyond traditional asado.

1. **Elena Restaurant**
   - **Location**: Four Seasons Hotel, Retiro, Posadas 1086/88
   - **Description**: Elena is a sophisticated restaurant serving contemporary Argentine cuisine with an emphasis on prime cuts of beef and seasonal ingredients. It is known for its impressive charcuterie and cheese selection.
   - **Pricing**: Main courses range from $40 to $90.
   - **Website**: www.fourseasons.com/buenosaires/dining/restaurants/elena
2. **Aramburu**
   - **Location**: Monserrat, Salta 1050
   - **Description**: Chef Gonzalo Aramburu's eponymous restaurant offers a 12-course tasting menu that combines molecular gastronomy techniques with traditional Argentine flavors. The experience is immersive, with an open kitchen that allows diners to watch the chefs in action.
   - **Pricing**: Tasting menu starts at $120 per person.
   - **Website**: www.arambururesto.com
3. **Chila**
   - **Location**: Puerto Madero, Alicia Moreau de Justo 1160
   - **Description**: One of Buenos Aires' most celebrated fine dining establishments, Chila serves innovative dishes inspired by Argentine cuisine, focusing on locally sourced ingredients. Its tasting menu changes seasonally.
   - **Pricing**: Tasting menu starts at $130 per person.
   - **Website**: www.chilaweb.com.ar

Spa and Wellness Retreats

For relaxation and rejuvenation, Buenos Aires has world-class spas offering an array of wellness treatments.

1. **Ahín Wellness & Spa – Palacio Duhau – Park Hyatt**
   - **Location**: Recoleta, Avenida Alvear 1661
   - **Description**: This luxury spa offers a variety of treatments, including massages, facials, and hydrotherapy. The tranquil setting and top-notch services make it an ideal escape from the city's hustle.

- **Pricing**: Treatments start at $150.
- **Website**: www.hyatt.com

2. **The Spa at Faena Hotel**
   - **Location**: Puerto Madero, Martha Salotti 445
   - **Description**: The Faena's spa draws on ancient healing practices and modern techniques, offering unique treatments such as a Tierra Santa ritual that combines steam, mud, and heat therapies.
   - **Pricing**: Signature treatments range from $200 to $400.
   - **Website**: www.faena.com/buenos-aires/spa

3. **Cielo Spa – Hotel Madero**
   - **Location**: Puerto Madero, Rosario Vera Peñaloza 360
   - **Description**: Cielo Spa offers a range of treatments, including massages, facials, and body wraps. The spa's rooftop location provides stunning views, enhancing the relaxation experience.
   - **Pricing**: Treatments start at $100.
   - **Website**: www.hotelmadero.com

Chapter 14: Practical Travel Tips

Traveling to Buenos Aires can be an enriching experience, offering a blend of culture, history, and vibrant city life. However, like any destination, it's important to be prepared with practical information to ensure a safe, enjoyable, and seamless visit. This chapter covers essential tips for staying safe, managing finances, staying connected, understanding local etiquette, and accessing emergency services.

Safety Tips for Tourists

Buenos Aires is generally a safe city for tourists, but as with any major city, there are safety concerns to be aware of. Here are some key tips to help you stay safe:

1. **Beware of Pickpockets**
   - In busy areas like **Florida Street**, **San Telmo Market**, or **La Boca**, pickpocketing can occur. Be mindful of your belongings, especially in crowded places or on public transportation.
   - Use anti-theft bags, keep valuables in front pockets, and avoid displaying expensive items like jewelry, cameras, or large sums of cash.
2. **Avoid Flashing Valuables**
   - Don't walk around with your smartphone or camera in hand. Keep them secured in your bag when not in use.
   - At night, especially in less crowded areas, avoid using your phone on the street or withdrawing cash from ATMs.
3. **Stick to Safe Areas**
   - While areas like **Recoleta**, **Palermo**, and **Puerto Madero** are generally safe, some neighborhoods, particularly in the southern parts of the city like **Constitución** and parts of **La Boca**, can be less secure, especially at night. It's best to explore La Boca during the daytime and stick to well-visited spots like **El Caminito**.
   - If you're going out late, consider using ride-sharing services like **Uber** or **Cabify** instead of public transport.
4. **Use Ride-Sharing Apps**
   - Taxi scams are not uncommon. Using apps like **Uber**, **Cabify**, or **BA Taxi** (the city's official taxi app) can reduce the risk of overcharging or detours.
5. **Stay Alert to Scams**
   - Common scams include fake currency exchanges (receiving counterfeit money) and the "mustard scam," where someone squirts a substance like

mustard or ketchup on you, then offers to help clean it up while stealing your belongings.
- Always check the bills you receive for authenticity, especially from street vendors or taxis.

6. **Emergency Numbers**
    - The emergency number in Argentina is **911** for police, fire, and medical assistance.
    - For a more direct line to tourist police, call **0800-999-5000**.

Currency Exchange and Banking Information

Argentina's financial situation can be complex, with fluctuating exchange rates and the existence of both official and unofficial (blue) exchange markets. Here's how to navigate currency matters in Buenos Aires:

1. **Currency and Exchange Rates**
    - The official currency is the **Argentine Peso (ARS)**. Banknotes come in denominations of 10, 20, 50, 100, 200, 500, 1,000, and 2,000 pesos.
    - Due to inflation, exchange rates can fluctuate significantly. To get the most current rate, use an app like **XE Currency** or visit websites like DolarHoy.

2. **Official vs. Blue Market Exchange Rates**
    - The **blue market rate** is an unofficial exchange rate that can be significantly higher than the official rate. Many tourists choose to exchange their U.S. dollars or euros at blue market rates for better value.
    - **Calle Florida** in the city center is known for offering blue market exchanges, but be cautious and use reputable "cuevas" (exchange houses). Alternatively, some hotels or trusted locals can direct you to reliable exchangers.

3. **Using ATMs**
    - ATMs can have high fees (often $10-15 USD per transaction) and may not always offer favorable exchange rates. If you must use an ATM, withdraw the maximum amount allowed to reduce fees.
    - ATMs affiliated with banks like **Banco Galicia**, **Banco Santander**, or **BBVA** are generally the most reliable.

4. **Credit Cards and Payment Apps**
    - Credit cards are widely accepted in Buenos Aires, especially in tourist areas. However, smaller shops or local markets may prefer cash.
    - **Mercado Pago** is a popular payment app that allows for cashless transactions in many stores. It's worth downloading if you plan to stay in Argentina for an extended period.

5. **Currency Exchange Locations**

- **Banco Nación** at **Ezeiza Airport**: Provides official exchange services with slightly better rates than some city locations.
- **Western Union**: Offers transfers that often provide the blue market rate. Sending money to yourself and picking it up in pesos can be a favorable way to access cash.
- **Cueva Buenos Aires** (Various Locations): Recommended for exchanging currency at the blue market rate. Always verify the authenticity of bills received.

Internet Access, SIM Cards, and Wi-Fi Availability

Staying connected in Buenos Aires is relatively easy, with plenty of options for SIM cards, Wi-Fi hotspots, and internet cafes.

1. **Buying a SIM Card**
   - **Claro**, **Movistar**, and **Personal** are the main mobile carriers in Argentina. You can purchase a SIM card at airports, mobile carrier stores, or kiosks throughout the city.
   - Prices for SIM cards start at around **ARS 300-500** (roughly **$1-2 USD**) and data packages vary from **ARS 500-1000** for 2-5 GB of data.
   - You may need to present your passport when purchasing a SIM card.
2. **Wi-Fi Availability**
   - Free Wi-Fi is widely available in cafes, restaurants, and public spaces like **Plaza de Mayo** or **Recoleta Park**.
   - Many hotels and accommodations offer free Wi-Fi, though speeds can vary.
   - **Public Wi-Fi hotspots** are available throughout the city, but for security reasons, avoid conducting sensitive transactions (like online banking) on public networks.
3. **Internet Cafes**
   - Internet cafes are becoming less common due to widespread Wi-Fi access, but you can still find a few in areas like **Microcentro** or **San Telmo**.
4. **Mobile Hotspot Rentals**
   - If you prefer consistent internet access, consider renting a portable Wi-Fi device from companies like **Travel WiFi Argentina**.
   - Rental prices typically start at **$5-8 USD per day**, depending on data requirements.

Etiquette and Cultural Considerations

Understanding the local customs and etiquette in Buenos Aires can help you navigate social situations and avoid inadvertently offending anyone. Here's a guide to help you fit in:

1. **Greetings**
   - Argentinians typically greet with a **cheek kiss** on the right cheek, even when meeting for the first time.
   - When addressing someone, use formal titles like **Señor**, **Señora**, or **Señorita**, unless given permission to use their first name.

2. **Dining Etiquette**
   - **Meal Times**: Lunch is usually around 1-3 p.m., and dinner often starts late, around 9-10 p.m. Don't be surprised if restaurants are empty at traditional dining hours.
   - **Sharing Mate**: Drinking **mate** (a traditional herbal tea) is a social activity. The host typically prepares the mate and shares it in a specific order, refilling it for each person. If offered, take a sip and pass it back to the host.
   - **Tipping**: Although tipping is not obligatory, it is customary to leave a **10% tip** for good service at restaurants.

3. **Social Norms**
   - **Personal Space**: Argentinians are more physically expressive and may stand closer during conversations than people from other cultures. This isn't considered invasive, but rather a sign of friendliness.
   - **Dress Code**: Buenos Aires is a fashion-conscious city, and locals tend to dress smartly. While casual wear is acceptable, wearing slightly more refined clothing can help you blend in better.

4. **Conversation Topics**
   - **Soccer (Fútbol)**: A passionate topic for many locals. If you're a fan, discussing teams like **Boca Juniors** or **River Plate** can spark interesting conversations.
   - **Politics and Economics**: These topics can be sensitive, especially concerning Argentina's financial situation. Approach them with caution.

Emergency Contacts and Health Services

In the event of an emergency, knowing who to contact and where to go is crucial. Buenos Aires has a reliable network of emergency services and healthcare facilities.

1. **Emergency Numbers**
   - **911**: For all emergencies, including police, fire, and medical assistance.
   - **0800-999-5000**: Tourist police hotline.
   - **107**: Ambulance and medical emergencies.
2. **Hospitals and Clinics**
   - **Hospital Alemán** (Recoleta): Known for quality care and English-speaking staff.
     - **Location**: Avenida Pueyrredón 1640
     - **Website**: www.hospitalaleman.org.ar
   - **Hospital Británico** (Barracas): Offers comprehensive medical services and a good reputation for treating foreigners.
     - **Location**: Perdriel 74
     - **Website**: www.hospitalbritanico.org.ar
   - **Sanatorio Güemes** (Palermo): Another well-regarded facility for healthcare.
     - **Location**: Francisco Acuña de Figueroa 1235
     - **Website**: www.sg.org.ar
3. **Pharmacies (Farmacias)**
   - Pharmacies are widespread throughout Buenos Aires. Look for signs that say "**Farmacia**," and note that some operate 24/7.
   - Common chains include **Farmacity** and **Dr. Ahorro**.
4. **Travel Insurance**
   - It is highly recommended to have travel insurance that covers medical emergencies, especially if you plan to engage in adventure activities or are staying for an extended period.

Chapter 15: Buenos Aires Essentials

Buenos Aires is a vibrant city with rich cultural history, beautiful neighborhoods, and unique attractions. When preparing for a trip to Buenos Aires, it's important to have practical travel information to navigate the city efficiently, stay safe, and make the most of your experience. This chapter covers essential tips, tools, and resources for travelers visiting the Argentine capital.

Key Phone Numbers and Emergency Services

In case of emergencies or urgent situations, it's essential to have the right contacts at hand.

- **Emergency Services**:
    - **General Emergency (Police, Ambulance, Fire)**: 911
    - **Tourist Police (Assistance in English)**: +54 11 4346 5748
    - **Medical Emergencies (SAME Ambulance Service)**: 107
    - **Fire Department**: 100
    - **National Road Safety (For traffic accidents)**: 0800 122 2678
- **Useful Contacts**:
    - **U.S. Embassy in Buenos Aires**: +54 11 5777 4533
    - **British Embassy in Buenos Aires**: +54 11 4808 2200
    - **Tourist Information Center**: +54 11 5030 9200
    - **Lost and Found (Subway)**: +54 11 3220 3600

It's a good idea to write these numbers down or save them on your phone for easy access.

Travel Apps to Download Before Your Trip

Several travel apps can significantly enhance your Buenos Aires experience by providing real-time information, transportation options, and local recommendations.

1. **Transportation Apps**:
    - **BA Cómo Llego**: This app helps navigate public transportation, providing directions for buses, subways, and walking routes.
        - **Website**: BA Cómo Llego
    - **SUBE App**: Allows users to check the balance on their SUBE transportation card, recharge it, and find nearby places to add credit.
        - **Website**: SUBE App
    - **Cabify and Uber**: Popular ride-sharing services. Cabify is often preferred for its reliability and local knowledge.

2. **Navigation Apps**:
   - **Google Maps**: Reliable for directions and transportation options, including bus and subway routes.
   - **Maps.me**: Offers offline maps, useful when navigating areas with limited internet connectivity.
3. **Local Recommendations and Dining Apps**:
   - **Restorando**: Helps find and book tables at restaurants across Buenos Aires, including trendy spots in Palermo and Recoleta.
   - **Guía Oleo**: A restaurant guide with user reviews, covering everything from high-end dining to local "parrillas" (steakhouses).
4. **Translation and Language Apps**:
   - **Google Translate**: Has an offline Spanish-English dictionary and voice translation.
   - **Duolingo**: A fun way to learn basic Spanish phrases before and during your trip.
5. **Entertainment and Event Apps**:
   - **Tango BA**: Provides information on tango shows, milongas (dance venues), and classes in Buenos Aires.
   - **Cultura Buenos Aires**: Lists cultural events, festivals, and exhibitions in the city.

Packing Checklist for Every Season

Buenos Aires has a temperate climate, but the weather can vary widely depending on the time of year. Here's a packing guide for each season:

1. **Summer (December to February)**:
   - **Clothing**: Lightweight, breathable clothes (cotton, linen), sandals, and a hat for sun protection.
   - **Sun Protection**: Sunscreen, sunglasses, and a reusable water bottle.
   - **Additional Items**: A light sweater or jacket for cooler nights.
2. **Autumn (March to May)**:
   - **Clothing**: Light layers such as long-sleeve shirts, a light jacket, and comfortable pants.
   - **Footwear**: Comfortable walking shoes for exploring the city.
   - **Rain Gear**: An umbrella or rain jacket, especially for late autumn.
3. **Winter (June to August)**:
   - **Clothing**: Warm clothing, including sweaters, a medium-weight coat, and a scarf. While winters are mild compared to other destinations, temperatures can drop to around 6°C (43°F) at night.

- o **Footwear**: Waterproof shoes or boots for wet days.
- o **Accessories**: Gloves and a hat for extra warmth.
4. **Spring (September to November)**:
   - o **Clothing**: Similar to autumn, with layers that can be added or removed as temperatures fluctuate.
   - o **Sun Protection**: Sunscreen and sunglasses, as the spring sun can be strong.
   - o **Footwear**: Comfortable walking shoes.

Local Customs and Holidays

Understanding the cultural norms and important holidays can greatly enhance your experience in Buenos Aires.

1. **Local Customs**:
   - o **Greetings**: It's common to greet people with a kiss on the cheek, even when meeting for the first time. In formal settings, a handshake is also appropriate.
   - o **Tipping**: While not mandatory, tipping 10% in restaurants is customary. Tipping for good service at hotels and by taxi drivers is also appreciated.
   - o **Mate Drinking**: "Mate" is a traditional herbal drink enjoyed throughout Argentina. Sharing mate is a social activity, and it's considered polite to accept a sip if offered.
   - o **Dinnertime**: Argentinians eat late, with dinner often starting at 9 PM or later. Most restaurants don't get busy until after 8 PM.
2. **Major Holidays and Festivals**:
   - o **New Year's Day (January 1st)**: Celebrated with family gatherings and fireworks.
   - o **Carnival (February/March)**: Buenos Aires hosts parades and performances. Dates vary each year.
   - o **Malvinas Day (April 2nd)**: Commemorates the fallen soldiers of the Falklands War.
   - o **Independence Day (July 9th)**: A national holiday with parades and celebrations.
   - o **Day of Tradition (November 10th)**: Celebrates Argentine culture and folk traditions, including gaucho lifestyle and traditional dances.
   - o **Christmas (December 25th)**: Christmas in Buenos Aires features family gatherings, fireworks, and midnight celebrations.

Chapter 16: Final Thoughts and Reflections

Buenos Aires is a city that captures the heart and soul of Argentina. Its blend of European charm, Latin American vibrancy, and a dynamic cultural scene make it an unforgettable travel destination. Here are some final thoughts and tips to help you make the most of your time in the city.

Making the Most of Your Buenos Aires Trip

To fully embrace Buenos Aires, consider spending time exploring its various neighborhoods, attending cultural events, and trying the local cuisine.

- **Embrace the City's Rhythm**: Don't rush your trip. Take the time to enjoy leisurely meals, walk through local markets, and soak in the sights. Buenos Aires' beauty lies in the small details – from the architecture to the street performers.
- **Experience the Tango**: Whether you're a dancer or just an observer, tango is an essential part of Buenos Aires' culture. Attend a show at **Café de los Angelitos** or take a tango class at **La Catedral Club** to dive deeper into this iconic dance.
- **Explore on Foot**: Some of the best experiences happen when you wander without a specific destination. Stroll through neighborhoods like **Palermo** and **San Telmo**, where you'll find unexpected gems like street art, antique shops, and cozy cafés.

Tips for Discovering Hidden Gems

While there are popular attractions that every visitor should see, Buenos Aires has many lesser-known spots that offer a deeper understanding of the city.

- **Villa Crespo's Murals**: Explore the street art scene in **Villa Crespo**, where murals tell stories of local history, politics, and culture.
- **El Zanjón de Granados**: A fascinating archaeological site and underground labyrinth that dates back to the 18th century, located in **San Telmo**.
  - **Website**: http://www.elzanjon.com.ar
- **Chacarita Cemetery**: Less famous than Recoleta, but equally interesting, with ornate tombs and the resting place of tango legend **Carlos Gardel**.
- **Secret Speakeasies**: Hidden bars like **The Harrison Speakeasy** require a password for entry and offer unique cocktails.

Embracing the Spirit of Buenos Aires

Buenos Aires is more than just a city; it's a lifestyle. Its people are passionate, the culture is expressive, and the streets are always alive with music, art, and conversation.

- **Connect with the Locals**: Argentinians are warm and friendly. Engage with them, ask for recommendations, or join a conversation in a café. It's a great way to learn about the city's hidden spots and local culture.
- **Enjoy the Nightlife**: Buenos Aires has a vibrant nightlife that goes well beyond clubs. Visit a **peña folklórica** to hear traditional music or attend a late-night film screening at one of the city's independent cinemas.

Planning Your Next Argentine Adventure

After experiencing Buenos Aires, consider exploring other regions of Argentina. The country offers diverse landscapes, from the icy peaks of **Patagonia** to the arid deserts of **Salta**.

- **Iguazú Falls**: Located on the border with Brazil, this natural wonder is a must-see for travelers who love breathtaking landscapes.
- **Mendoza**: Famous for its vineyards, Mendoza is the place to go for wine lovers. Enjoy wine tastings and tours in the Andes foothills.
- **Bariloche**: A picturesque town in Patagonia, known for its Swiss-like architecture, ski resorts, and hiking trails.

By understanding the essentials and embracing the unique aspects of Buenos Aires, you can ensure a trip that is not only memorable but also insightful and enriching.

Made in the USA
Columbia, SC
18 December 2024

49952195R00057